THE COMPLETE STEP-BY-STEP
WATERCOLOUR
COURSE

THE COMPLETE STEP-BY-STEP
WATERCOLOUR
COURSE

Michael Whittlesea

CHANCELLOR
PRESS

Executive Managers	Kelly Flynn
	Susan Egerton-Jones
Editors	Christian Bailey, Sandy Shepherd
Art Editor	Ruth Levy
Production	Peter Phillips
General Assistant	Tracey Mead

The author and creators of this book are
particularly grateful to the following
artists for their generous contributions:
Charles Bartlett, R. Dent, Harry Eccleston,
Charlotte Halliday, Diana Johnson, Chris Jones,
Pamela Kay, Anne Maclaren, Juliette Palmer,
Polly Raynes, Jackie Rizvi, Dennis Roxby Bott,
Annie Williams, Lucy Willis and Albany Wiseman.

Previously published under the title *The Complete Watercolour Course*
by the Artists House Division of Mitchell Beazley International Ltd,
part of Reed International Books

This edition published in 1992 by
Chancellor Press, Michelin House, 81 Fulham Road,
London SW3 6RB

© Reed International Books Ltd 1987

ISBN 1 85152 228 X

Printed in Malaysia

CONTENTS

INTRODUCTION

There can be few things which are more unpredictable or satisfying than painting in watercolour. The simple freshness of the medium, its brilliance and sparkle, have fascinated painters for centuries.

This watercolour course provides a guide to readily obtainable materials and practical information which will enable you to make a start and to develop your skills.

You will not find a catalogue of tricks here but an encouragement to use watercolour in a spontaneous and creative way, a straightforward, informal guide to the many methods and techniques of watercolour painting which will help you to paint on paper what you see.

After mastering the basics, you are taken step-by-step through the stages that demonstrate simply how to paint accomplished pictures and how to express your own imagination and talent. The clear instructions will help you to develop and refine your skills in this fascinating medium.

Still-lifes, landscapes, figures, buildings and animals are all covered in the easy-to-follow text and illustrations, and a glossary at the end of the book defines the technical terms used.

There are no hard and fast rules in the successful use of watercolour — this most versatile of media. It is the purpose of this book to encourage readers to discover for themselves the pleasures of painting in watercolour, and to develop styles and, indeed, techniques to suit each of them individually.

Michael Whittlesea

HISTORY AND BACKGROUND

Watercolour is one of the oldest painting media known to artists. It was used as a basis for cave paintings, medieval manuscripts and studies for many of the greatest paintings in the world. The picture-making problems, drawing, composition and techniques, were just as important to the artist in the past as they are to today's painter. To the beginner, a blank sheet of paper can be a terrifying thing, and the first washes of colour are a big step. It can be helpful and encouraging to look back at the work of previous centuries.

More than ten thousand years ago cave artists used colours made from earth and chalk pigments of ochres, browns and reds, bound with gum or egg white, and then diluted with water. Black was obtained by taking burnt wood and bones, breaking and grinding them up to a powder, and mixing the result with water. With these basic pigments, ancient man drew animals and events on the walls of his caves. Many of these cave paintings have survived, for example at Lascaux, France.

Ancient Egyptian artists used water-based pigments on plaster to decorate tombs; medieval illuminators created and decorated manuscripts using watercolour; and Michelangelo's ceiling in the Sistine Chapel is probably one of the largest and greatest watercolours ever painted, the supreme example of water-based paints used in a grand functional manner.

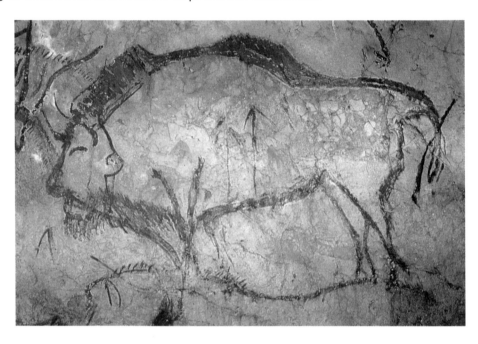

Albrecht Dürer (1471–1528), who lived and worked in northern Europe, used watercolour delicately, in thin washes of colour, to give his drawings substance and clarity. The lines of his underlying drawings were never lost — even the lightest marks are visible.

Above: a cave painting at Lascaux, France, painted by early cavemen more than 10,000 years ago, in which earth colours, such as ochres and browns, and black made from burnt wood and bones were used mixed with water.
Left: this flower painting was drawn by the German artist and engraver Albrecht Dürer, one of the first artists to employ thin washes of watercolour over a drawing done in painstaking detail and fine lines.

For many years watercolour was used for studies, roughs and sketches for large, usually commissioned, oil paintings. Both Rubens (1577–1640) and Rembrandt (1606–1669) made hundreds of mainly monochromatic sketches in watercolour. Sometimes the paper would first be tinted overall with grey or yellow ochre in the studio. Once it was dry, the artist, working out of doors or with a model, would brush in the outlines with sepia. Using a single colour is an advantage when you have to work with speed.

Classical watercolour came into its own during the 18th century, when the value of watercolour as a medium in its own right was recognized. The main characteristic of the paint that attracted artists then was its transparency, which allows the white of the paper to shine through the colour.

In the best works from that time, subtle and interesting variations were produced as the first brush marks were made and then clarified. No matter how detailed and complex, good watercolours retain a definable freshness. These

qualities are apparent in landscapes of the 18th-century school of English watercolourists: John Crome (1768–1821), John Varley (1778–1842), John Sell Cotman (1788–1842) and Thomas Girtin (1775–1802).

Their mistakes and struggles are just as interesting as their successes and their pictorial problems were no different from the difficulties encountered by watercolourists today.

Top: this sepia drawing of a girl resting, by Rembrandt, shows his wonderful ability to draw quickly with a brush.
Above left: in this painting of Greta Bridge, done in 1807, the English artist John Sell Cotman made full use of the luminous qualities of watercolour in an instinctive, boldly designed painting.
Left: Thomas Girtin, born in 1775, succeeded in painting remarkable pictures with a very limited palette. By superimposing washes of colour, he produced rich paintings from as few as five colours.

Towards the end of the 18th century, and during the early 19th, watercolour painting extended in several directions and was used in an extraordinary way by the eccentric English visionaries William Blake (1757–1827) and Samuel Palmer (1805–1881). Blake produced disturbing and imaginative pictures and Palmer, influenced by him, painted dreams and visions of strange gardens and landscapes.

But it was John Constable (1776–1837) who captured the atmospheric quality of the moment with his Suffolk landscapes painted in a direct powerful manner. JMW Turner (1775–1851) also produced brilliant images in watercolour, of Venice, seascapes and storms. Turner painted with passion and conviction, pushing and splashing the paint until it produced the effects he wanted.

The uses and advantages of watercolour were not, of course, only appreciated by the English. Paul Cézanne (1839–1906) used watercolour for still-life, figures and landscapes. And it was his work, painted at the end of the

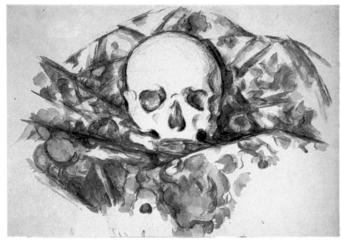

Top: *Stonehenge* by John Constable, whose watercolours are considered by many people to be more successful than the major oil paintings they were sketched for.
Above and right: Paul Cézanne painted these two very different pictures. The still-life with a skull is a very disturbing and powerful painting whereas the landscape is tranquil and soothing. Both pictures show abstract qualities, a sense of pattern, colour and tone. Above all there is a remarkable sense of structure in which the white paper has been left to unify the composition.

Opposite, top: this abstract painting in watercolour by Wassily Kandinsky was painted in 1910. It is one of the first abstract paintings that was produced in watercolour.
Far right: Edward Hopper's *The Mansard Roof* shows the brooding, poetic realism of his work. He used the effects of light and shadow to great advantage to become one of the major realist painters of the 20th century.

19th century, which was to influence so much of 20th-century painting.

Wassily Kandinsky (1866–1944) painted some of the first abstract paintings in watercolour, and early 20th-century expressionist painters such as the German painter Emil Nolde (1867–1956) found the unpredictable quality of watercolour, its brilliance and immediacy, an ideal medium for expressionism. As Paul Klee (1879–1940) discovered, watercolour was ideal for his images of a dream world.

Watercolour painting has flourished in the United States. Edward Hopper (1882–1967) studied in Europe and was influenced by the work of the Post-impressionists. Returning to the United States, he painted haunting urban landscapes with a wonderful feeling of light and shadow. The American watercolour tradition continues with Andrew Wyeth (1917–).

The limitations of watercolour have in recent years been reduced by the use of masking tapes and fluids. Airbrushes, too, can produce results unlike anything that has been painted before although they are mainly used by graphic artists for commercial projects.

MATERIALS AND BASIC TECHNIQUES

One of the joys of watercolour is that it requires few materials — a selection of brushes, colours and papers and, of course, water. But it is knowing exactly what kind of materials are best for your purposes that is difficult. In the first section you will learn about the basic materials and equipment, the different kinds of watercolour paints, the best colours to start off with, what papers and brushes to use, and whether you need an easel.

An essential part of watercolour painting is preparing your paper; here you are shown how to stretch your paper before using it.

Once you have the wherewithal to paint, how do you go about it? In the second section, some basic techniques are illustrated to get you acquainted with the medium. But in addition, several experimental techniques are demonstrated to give you a tantalizing taste of the exciting potential of this beautiful medium.

MATERIALS AND EQUIPMENT

One of the many good things about watercolour painting is that it's easy to try out because you do not need a vast collection of expensive equipment and the only liquid required is tap water. Watercolour painting is simply making marks in colour on a surface, and some of the greatest paintings have been done with very basic and limited materials. Turner, for example, often painted with only five or six colours.

If you already have a selection of painting equipment, don't throw it away. All you need to make a good start is a simple, adequate selection of brushes and paints. Then, with a bit of experience, you can widen your scope.

There is a vast selection of watercolour equipment readily available, in fact a bewildering choice. Years ago, a young artist would serve an apprenticeship with an established painter and learn to grind and mix colours, prepare surfaces to work on and to make brushes. In the 20th century everything we need is manufactured.

Sometimes the labels are difficult to read and it's a problem to know what you can use the materials for. Often, the chances are you don't need them. For financial and practical reasons the real problem is what to do without.

The moment you work out of doors, or have to carry your equipment across a muddy field, you very quickly discover what you can do without. When you are working under pressure, your painting equipment must be simple and functional.

With time, knowledge and awareness about the range of materials will give you the confidence to exploit watercolour to its full extent. Part of the joy of painting is that, as you experiment, you will gradually develop your ability and discover the full potential of your materials, such as the pleasure of the first sumptuous wash on a piece of good watercolour paper.

It's a good idea to visit artists' suppliers to see what's new on the market. I always think of art supply shops as an Aladdin's cave, full of exciting and unexpected things to be tried out and experimented with. Sometimes, trying out paints or papers that you have previously regarded as unsuitable can produce interesting and unexpected results, which add to your experience.

Keeping it all very simple, the following sections describe and recommend a basic painting kit for the beginner: a few good colours, a decent brush and paper properly prepared. I have given very little space to making your own equipment; you are better advised to spend the time painting.

Water and Waterpots

Water is an obvious and essential ingredient of watercolour painting. Like easels, water and water containers come in two categories: indoor and outdoor.

For indoors, empty jam or mayonnaise jars are fine as long as they have a wide mouth. Yoghurt cartons are too small and light, and tip over easily. Some artists use two pots of water. One is kept very clean, for water that is added to the paint, and the other for cleaning brushes. This arrangement is good in theory but in practice I very soon forget which waterpot is which. In concentrating on what I am painting, I dip my brush in whichever jar is nearest. This sometimes also results in brushes being dipped into my coffee cup.

I collect jars that I think will be useful for waterpots, and make a regular point of throwing away dirty and stained pots.

On a painting trip, unless you know that there will be a constant source of clean water on site, take at least a pint of water with you. It makes sense to use plastic containers with a secure screw top. Camping suppliers have a good selection.

Besides paint, water, brushes and paper you will need the following essential items before you start:

- Putty/kneadable rubber or eraser (soft rubber will not spoil the surface of watercolour paper)

- Brown paper adhesive tape

- Scissors

- HB pencil and a soft 2B pencil

- Stanley knife or craft knife with replaceable blades

- A natural medium-sized sponge

- A box of white paper tissues, or for economy, large amounts of white toilet paper (*not* the coloured kind)

- A plastic or metal waste bin (piles of soggy rubbish are the inevitable result of watercolour experiments)

CHOOSING WATERCOLOUR PAINTS

The easiest way to start painting watercolours is to buy a watercolour box filled with preselected colours. It will probably come with a brush or two, so that with a piece of white paper and a jam jar full of tap water, you will be ready to paint. Even so, it is better to choose your own equipment. But the piles of watercolour equipment on display in art supply shops are pretty daunting. Where do you start when you only want a few of the right colours and brushes? And how do you avoid wasting money? Start by looking at the range of paints.

You will find that colours are manufactured mainly in four different types — small wrapped blocks of semi-moist paint, round buttons of dry watercolour, tubes of creamy paint and bottles of liquid colour.

There are two qualities, "Artists'" and "Students'". Your early results will be so much better with Artists' colours that buying the cheaper Students' is false economy. If you start with the best colours you can afford, the results, even if you can't draw very well, will be so much more exciting and the brilliance of the paint will encourage you to go on. Good colours are rich and highly saturated and can also be justified economically by spreading further. The pigments in them are ground very finely, mixed with gum arabic, glycerine and water.

The price is indicated by a series number. Some Artists' colours are more expensive than others. Inorganic pigments, for example, can cost very much more than the organic "earth" colours such as the ochres.

Watercolours are distinguished from other water-based paints by their transparency. "Poster colours" and "Designers' Gouache", although mixed with water, are opaque and used mainly for flat design work, not for painting watercolours.

Here are the details of the appearance and qualities of the four types of watercolour paint, and their containers, which you will find in your supply shop.

Pans and Half-pans
These are the small blocks of semi-moist wrapped watercolour. They fit into the sections of watercolour boxes which can be purchased separately. You choose the colours, take off the wrappers, and fit them into your watercolour box. Some metallic and plastic boxes are designed to work not only as a container but as a palette as well. Others have water reservoirs and bottles. Mahogany boxes, with metal liners, are the nicest to look at.

Buying colours in these blocks is economical and they are convenient to use out of doors. You don't waste time squeezing or pouring out paint. The colours are always in the same position in the box when you want them, and they don't leak.

The disadvantages are that it takes a little longer to lift the colour onto the brush, and it's irritating, once you have taken the wrapper off, to try and remember the name of the colour.

Watercolour paints come in four different forms: semi-moist pans and half-pans, which are convenient for outdoor use because they fit into a box in which they can also be mixed; dry cakes of paint; bottled liquid watercolours, which are useful for creating large areas of wash quickly; and tubes of paint, the most popular form.

Pan colours can dry out, so you may need to put a damp cloth over the pigments when they are not in use.

Dry Cakes

This form of watercolour usually consists of round, flat tablets. They look like brightly coloured buttons, arranged in boxes and come pre-selected and packaged.

The colour, although fairly concentrated, needs a lot of scrubbing with the brush before you can get enough pigment to start painting, which can be very frustrating. It's not my favourite form of watercolour. The only good thing about them is that they are inexpensive.

Tubes of Watercolour

Artists' watercolour in tubes is of very good quality. Some professional artists consider tubes to be a wasteful and expensive way of using watercolour. It's easy to squeeze out more than you need and the paint can leak and

solidify if the cap isn't replaced properly. There is a tendency for the colours to run together on the palette if you use too much water. It can also be a nuisance trying to identify and locate a particular colour among a pile of tubes whose labels have become torn and paint-stained.

Despite all this, tubes are my favourite form of watercolour. I keep them in an easily washable plastic container, using white plates and saucers to mix the colour on.

Squeezing the bright colours out onto a white plate first is a help, because, psychologically, starting to paint on a new piece of expensive watercolour paper can be extremely daunting.

Bottles of Liquid Watercolour

This is watercolour in a concentrated form, usually in bottles with a "dropper". Just a few drops in a saucer of water produces enough colour for a large expansive wash, so it is good for overall backgrounds when you need to use a

large brush. They are fragile and leaky to transport out of doors but good in the studio. However, there are snags. The colours tend to be rather vivid, more suitable for graphic designers and illustrators than watercolourists. Many of the colours act like dyes: one drop can indelibly sink into the paper and no amount of sponging or water will ever get it out.

Once you've decided which form of watercolour suits you, then select the colours. Too many colours are quite unnecessary and a hindrance. Better to start with a few basic pigments and extend and change as you gain experience.

A suggested palette

Alizarin crimson
A very intense, dark red which itself cannot be mixed from other colours, but when mixed with ultramarine, for example, produces a very dark mixture.

Yellow ochre
A very useful opaque "earth" colour used extensively in landscape painting. Mixed with blues, it produces greens that are quiet and not sharp and acid.

Cadmium red
A brilliant opaque colour; warm and very intense; when mixed with other colours it produces good pinks and purples.

Cadmium yellow
A strong, sharp yellow which has substance and covering power. Although expensive it can, mixed with other colours, produce a wide variety of rich colour and tone.

Light red
Terracotta in appearance, when diluted it can be used in the early stages of a painting, and then built up to produce a very solid colour.

Ultramarine
This mixes well with other colours to produce dark intense mixtures, excellent for backgrounds.

Viridian
A rather transparent colour which on its own is very sharp, but mixed with reds, pinks, yellows and browns produces cooler versions of each colour.

Raw sienna
A transparent colour, which has the appearance of a warm dark yellow. Less "earthy" than yellow ochre, it is very useful in painting the figure or portraits.

Cobalt blue
A light gentle blue, not as intense as ultramarine, but pale washes can be built up to produce a more intense colour.

Payne's grey
One of the most useful colours; dark blue in appearance, when it is mixed with other colours it can produce dark, intense shadows that are still full of colour.

PAPER

The most useful way to learn about the differences in the various specially made watercolour papers is to try them out, buying a sheet of each type. Papers vary a great deal, some are smooth, some rough and absorbent. Experiment to find out which paper suits you best. The character of watercolour paper, its surface texture, totally affects the look of a watercolour painting. It is stronger than most other papers, to allow for repeated soaking, sponging and repainting.

Watercolour paper can be either handmade or machinemade and this difference is reflected in the price. The best quality handmade paper is made from cotton rag, and has a low acidity level. High acid levels can affect the painted surface, discolouring it.

Papers are made in three surfaces, smooth, medium and rough, known technically as: hot pressed (H.P.); NOT (that is *not* hot pressed) or cold pressed (C.P.); and rough.

"H.P." Hot pressed paper has a smooth hard surface. Fine detail is easier to convey, but it has an unattractive slippery quality.

"NOT" is lightly cold pressed and has a medium texture, which is easy to handle.

"ROUGH" paper is heavily textured. A wash of watercolour on a rough surfaced paper will break up, giving a classic "watercolour" look. Precision and detail are difficult. It is mainly handmade.

There is a right and a wrong side of good papers, indicated by a watermark. If I have to abandon a watercolour, I will, if I haven't completely worn out the paper, turn it over and use the other side.

Paper can be bought in single sheets or in bulk (*see box*). There are blocks of ready-to-use paper which is gummed along the edges. When the painting is finished and dry, the top sheet can be separated and taken off by running a palette knife along the edges. There are also boards with watercolour paper ready mounted, and spiral-bound pads of paper. Ordinary cartridge/drawing paper, although good for drawing, is totally unsuitable for watercolour painting as it lacks strength and texture.

Sizes and weights of papers differ from country to country. It is still common practice for art suppliers to describe paper in the old Imperial sizes. For example, the most common size of watercolour paper is Imperial which measures 775×572rnm ($30\frac{1}{2} \times 22\frac{1}{2}$in). The weight of paper is indicated in grams per square metre (*see box*) or by pounds of paper per ream.

Weights and measures

Paper sizes and weights are normally metric but some papers are still measured in Imperial. Weight is measured in grams per square metre (gsm or gm², eg 100gsm — light, 640gsm — heavy) or in pounds per ream (eg 72 pounds — light, 300 pounds — heavy). The following table is a guide to Imperial sizes which individual makers supply in their own variation of size. "Domestic Etching" paper in N. America is supplied in sizes: 26×40in (66×101cm) and 20×26in (50×66cm).

Metric	Imperial
A0 841×1189mm	**Antiquarian** 53×31in (1346×787mm)
A1 594×841mm	**Double Elephant** $40 \times 26\frac{1}{4}$in (1016×679mm)
A2 420×594mm	**Imperial** $30\frac{1}{2} \times 22\frac{1}{2}$in ($775 \times 572$mm)
A3 279×420mm	**Double Crown** 30×20in (762×508mm)
A4 210×297mm	**Royal** 24×19in (610×483mm)
A5 148×210mm	**Medium** $22 \times 17\frac{1}{2}$in (559×444mm)

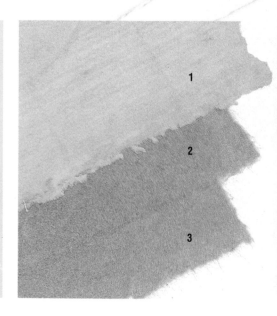

1

2

3

Drawing Boards

A half Imperial drawing board is just the right size for both indoor and outdoor painting. It is necessary to have a board that can cope with the pull and stress of stretching paper.

The best drawing boards are made from good quality softwood spruce, which takes up shrinkage and expansion. I find these are most suitable for watercolour painting. Gummed tape adheres easily and you can push drawing pins into it. Laminated boards are not suitable, because sticky paper tape does not adhere, nor are thin hardboard/Masonite or plywood boards because they cannot cope with the shrinkage and warping you get with stretching paper. And there is no need either to invest in an inclined tubular steel drawing board; it is just as easy to work on the kitchen table.

For outdoor sketching, weight and size are important factors. You don't want a drawing board that is longer than your arms. Working indoors, I make constant use of two large, thick and heavy chipboard drawing boards which would be too heavy to carry outside. Their only disadvantage is that the edges, even though primed with white undercoat, crumble with use.

As with other materials, you will collect boards of various sizes as you go on. I find it very useful to have a large collection of drawing boards, with paper stretched on both sides. When I cannot resolve a painting and it seems difficult to "finish" it, I place it on one side, face to the wall and work on another. After a few days or weeks, I can return to the board facing the wall, and can often clearly see what I should do to it.

1 **Fabriano Roma**
2 **Japanese Mingei**
3 **Japanese Mingei**
4 **Whatman Rough**
5 **Whatman NOT/C.P.**
6 **Whatman H.P.**
7 **Waterford Rough**
8 **Waterford NOT/C.P.**
9 **Waterford H.P.**
10 **Bockingford**
11 **Georgian**
12 **Cartridge/Drawing paper**
13 **Greens RWS Rough**
14 **Greens RWS NOT/C.P.**
15 **Greens RWS H.P.**
16 **Greens Camber Sand NOT/C.P.**
17 **Greens Turner Grey NOT/C.P.**
18 **Greens De Wint Rugged**

STRETCHING PAPER

Most papers will cockle and distort when they become wet and damp with watercolour. To avoid this, it is normal practice to stretch paper before starting to work on it. On very heavy papers, i.e. 250lbs or more, you can avoid stretching by securing the edges with large paper clips, the bulldog variety. This works well if the paper doesn't become too wet, but lighter papers always need stretching.

It is important to have everything you need near to hand before you start stretching paper. A drawing board (remember, hardboard is not suitable as it will buckle and bend); the watercolour paper trimmed all round to approximately 25mm (one inch) smaller than the drawing board; four strips of brown paper gummed tape, cut 50mm (two inches) longer than each side of the paper; a sponge and a bowl or glass of tap water.

1 Immerse the paper in cold water for a couple of minutes. I use the bath, which gives plenty of room and it's usually clean. Sinks always seem cramped and care must be taken to soak the paper evenly and not to damage it. Do not use hot water, it affects the "size" on the surface of the paper.

2 Hold the paper up and shake it to dislodge surplus water. Place the paper onto the board and make sure that it is perfectly flat. Working quickly, dampen the gum strip. Running it under the tap will make it too wet; you can use a sponge or lick it.

3 Stick the gummed paper strips around the outer eges of the paper, half their width on the board, half on the paper. As an extra precaution, you can push drawing pins into each corner, which will help to stop the paper wrinkling. As the paper dries, it will shrink and become taut.

4 The board should lie flat while the paper is drying. Leaning it against a radiator will result in the water draining to one side, and the paper will dry unevenly and pull off the board. Do not attempt to use stretched paper until it is dry. It's a good idea to stretch paper the night before you need it. This avoids the temptation to work on a semi-damp surface. I use at least six drawing boards at a time to stretch paper, leaving them to dry overnight. I then have a selection of stretched papers and can work on several paintings at once, going on to the next while waiting for one to dry.

It is possible to stretch paper of substantial weight when it is dry, in the same manner as canvas, using drawing pins around wooden stretchers. The paper becomes taut like a drum. The disadvantage is that when it becomes wet it is all too easy to put your brush through it.

CHOOSING AND CARING
FOR BRUSHES

You can use all sorts of tools to put paint onto paper — sponges, knives, tissues and even fingers — but the most commonly used instrument is the brush. It is a very important element in watercolour painting. You only need four or five brushes to start. Try to buy the best brushes, going for quality rather than quantity. Cheap brushes do not last and rarely give good results.

The best brushes are Russian Sable. The hair has a life and springiness lacking in other types of brushes. With reasonable care, they hold their shape and possess great strength.

Oxhair brushes are cheaper than sable but do not have that sureness of touch and reliability that sable has. I would rather spend money on small to medium-size sables and use oxhair for large-scale washes, where the cost of a very large sable brush would make it almost prohibitive.

The cheapest brushes are either synthetic or squirrel hair. Nylon brushes do not have as long a working life as sable. Squirrel always feels limp and, like a lot of less expensive brushes, loses its hair.

You need four or five brushes of different sizes and shapes because using the same brush can result in a monotonous surface. Manufacturers produce watercolour brushes in up to 13 or 14 different sizes, each of them numbered on the handle — low numbers for small, getting higher as the size increases. I suggest you start by purchasing round brushes in the following sizes: 1, 4, 7, 10 or 12. A brush for flat washes could be an economic oxhair, flat, wide and large.

The best brushes to start with are sable round brushes — you will need four or five. Use a large brush for laying on washes, and the thinner ones for detail.

Large wash brush

Size 8

Size 6

**Size 4
Lettering brush**

Size 2

Size 00

Because I think it's worthwhile to buy the very best sable brushes for most watercolour painting, I economize by using large, flat house-painting brushes for backgrounds.

Try out brushes before you purchase them. There should be a jar of water for this purpose in your art supply shop. Dip the brush into the water, shake it once, and the hairs of the brush should form a point. They should not stick out in the wrong direction. If the brush doesn't form a perfect shape, reject it and try another.

Care of Brushes

Brushes are expensive and should be looked after. Good, well cared for brushes won't shed hairs and are pleasanter to work with. Learning to paint is much more difficult with a brush that is moulting.

While you are still painting, try not to leave brushes standing in water. Don't use brushes to scrub at that last drop of paint on the palette, it wears them out. When you have finished painting, always rinse brushes in clean water, making sure that you have gently washed away any pigment near the metal ferrule.

After cleaning, reshape the brush by drawing the damp brush over the palm of your hand, moulding the hairs to a point. The unhealthy but most obvious way is to suck the brush to reshape it. Caution here; some pigments, particularly cadmium yellow, are toxic.

Lay the brushes down to dry, making sure the hairs are not bent or cramped, taking care to protect the tops. If you put wet brushes in a tightly fitting container, mildew will develop. Moths are very keen on good brushes, so if you need to store brushes for any length of time, mothballs will act as a deterrent.

When you need to transport brushes, it is easily and cheaply done by arranging them on a slightly longer and wider piece of cardboard, holding them in place by elastic bands. This simple device helps to protect the ends of your brushes.

In the studio, stand your brush tops uppermost in a jam jar or purpose-made earthenware brush vase. I use two flowerpots to hold brushes in.

When you are carrying your brushes with you, strap them to a piece of board longer and wider than the brushes, with elastic bands.

When buying a round paint brush make sure that its bristles taper to a fine point. Reject brushes on which the bristles stick out and which have a ferrule with a seam.

**38mm (1½ inch)
Flat wash brush**

BRUSH STROKES

Brushes have long handles enabling you to hold them in several different positions. Each brush can make a variety of marks. Try holding your brushes in different ways. If you are too self-conscious about it, the resulting strokes will be mannered, stiff and unnatural but experience will soon loosen you up. Most professional painters never give a thought to how they hold a brush, nor even which brush to use. With practice, you will learn to pick up the right brush without even thinking about it. You can hold the brush as you would hold a pen to write a letter, or between the thumb and forefinger with the handle lying under the palm.

It is a good idea to try different brush techniques on various papers, as surface affects the marks you make. A non-absorbent paper acts differently from a wet, soaked surface. Practice will soon help you to know what proportion of pigment to water is required. Remember, a dry brush will make a very different mark from a loaded wet brush, and pressing hard will produce a different result from a light pressure.

Four strokes of colour laid side by side and allowed to merge and combine.

A "dry brush" with barely diluted pigment, dragged from side to side.

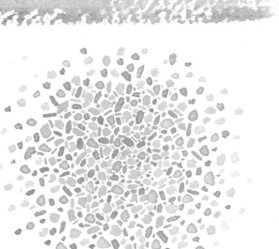

The point of a fine sable brush creates a delicate flecked effect by laying dots of colour side by side.

A long brush stroke applied with heavy pressure at first, then light pressure as the brush is lifted from the paper while the hand is still moving.

You will find that long strokes are produced in a very different way from short strokes, and that the way you sweep the brush across the paper, and the amount of paint on the brush, will dictate the length of the stroke. Painting a long stroke is not dissimilar to a golf or tennis follow-through. Keep your hand and arm moving, before, during and after the brush stroke. Don't attempt to correct anything.

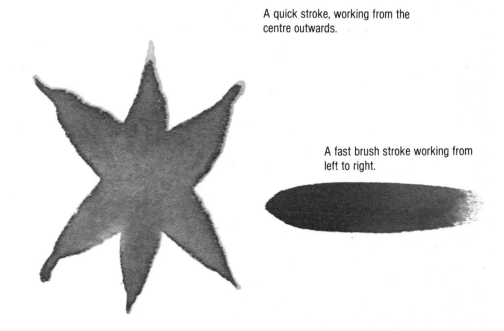

A quick stroke, working from the centre outwards.

A fast brush stroke working from left to right.

Compare a large, flat, long brush stroke with a fine line drawn by a fine sable. Experiment with slow strokes and fast strokes, and strokes from both left and right. Drag the brush with a scrubbing motion in different directions. Try squashing the loaded brush onto the paper.

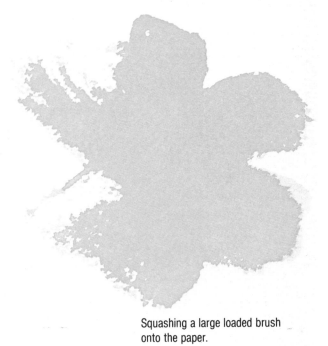

Squashing a large loaded brush onto the paper.

Scrubbing the brush in different directions.

Short strokes are produced by simply laying the head of a loaded brush onto the paper. Lift the brush up after a second or two. Don't go back to touch up the mark you have made.

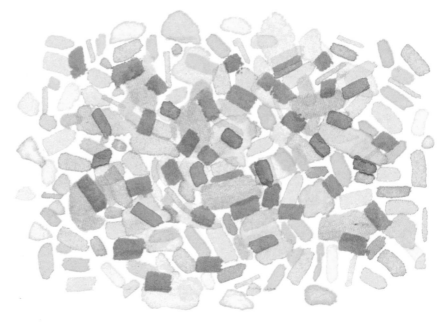

Short dabs of colour can vary in size, shape and direction.

Downward brush strokes overlaid by upward strokes.

Laying an overloaded fine brush onto the paper, letting it fall and roll.

Short strokes of colour. The loaded brush gently laid onto the paper, then lifted up after a couple of seconds.

A loaded brush, held gently at the top of the handle, slowly swept from left to right.

Broad strokes of wash are achieved by a loaded brush being in contact with the paper until the brush runs dry. More pigment can be applied by dipping the brush back into the colour and quickly connecting the first brush stroke with the second, using a continuous, circular, meandering movement. Keep your brush on the paper as much as you can. Try not to smooth out paint once it reaches the paper. The way it dries is part of the fascination of watercolour painting. You must not expect a fixed code of brush strokes. Certain marks will not necessarily describe a cloud or a tree. With time you will learn control of all the strokes a brush can make, and acquire an instinctive awareness of their uses and potential.

Broad stroke of colour using a meandering movement with a fully loaded brush.

Scrubbing the brush in an up and down movement.

EASELS

Easels can be expensive and it may be that you do not need one. Careful thought about your working preferences and locations will be worthwhile. A little experience of painting both indoors and out of doors will quickly help you to decide whether you need an easel or not.

Ask yourself the basic questions. Do you prefer to stand or sit while painting? Where do you mainly work, on a windy hillside or in a studio? I often simply lay a drawing board flat on the ground to work. Sitting cross-legged on walls or rocks, with the board in front of me, I have no need for an easel and I like the freedom to improvise on site. Carrying and erecting an easel can be an unnecessary hindrance.

If, after a little work both outside and inside, you feel an easel would be an advantage, ask your art supplier to let you fold up and erect a whole range of easels. If an easel is difficult and complicated to erect in an art shop, it's not going to be any easier outdoors.

A portable easel for outdoor sketching is harder to choose than a studio easel. It must be light enough to carry and yet be tough, robust and very stable in windy conditions.

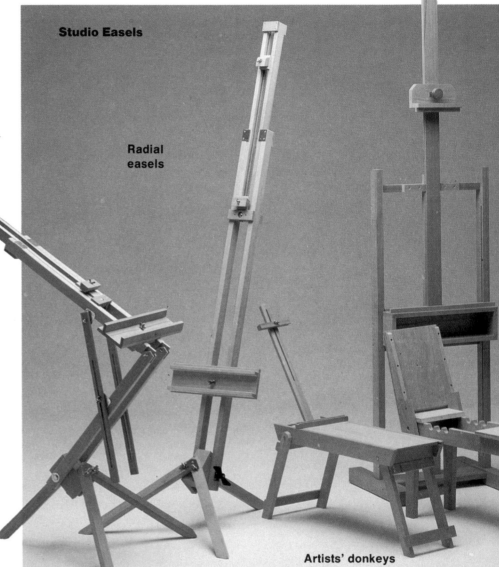

Studio Easels

Radial easels

Artists' donkeys

Manufacturers produce portable sketching easels in both metal and wood. Most have telescopic legs which allow you to paint standing or sitting down. Wooden sketching easels only weigh about 1.5kg (2–3lbs), so carrying them isn't the problem. The difficulty is instability and fragility. Even though the legs have small spikes to sink into the ground, the easels still tend to be unstable in gusty weather conditions.

Lightweight metal easels can be just as fragile. The telescopic legs are easily dented, and cease to function properly. Again, the metal easels do not give a stable working support.

One good feature possible on a sketching easel is a built-in paintbox, conveniently positioned below the drawing board. Another is a combined seat and easel. They also come with drawing boards that adjust to both horizontal and vertical positions. A handle is provided so that it's easy to carry when folded.

There is a larger and heavier easel which forms a solid drawing table when it's unfolded.

These wooden easels are probably too bulky to carry far, but if your preoccupation is painting in the garden or just outside the back door, this type of easel is very good for watercolour painting. With the paper in a horizontal position, you can lay very wet washes without the risk of the watercolour flowing and running down the paper. Wooden easels, especially if used out of doors, need plenty of furniture wax to prevent warping and distortion.

Studio easels are less of a problem. They range from small table top easels, not unlike a lectern, to very large, very heavy easels on wheels. The lightest table top easel is made of aluminium, not very stable and easily toppled over. The best table top easel is made of hardwood and as mobility isn't important, but stability is, it's wise to buy the most robust and solid table top easel you can find.

Artists' "Donkeys" are certainly sturdy and will last a lifetime. They resemble a wooden bench seat with a recess for your paints, and an upright support for the drawing board. They are excellent if you prefer to sit in the studio and paint with the paper in a vertical position.

The most favoured easel among artists is probably the "Studio Radial", very often used in the life classes of art colleges. It is tough and well made, folds up, but is too heavy to carry far. Some of the Radial easels have the added attraction of a central joint, which means you can tilt half the easel backwards, placing the drawing board in a horizontal position. (It's still easy to reach the paper when sitting.) Radial easels should last for a very long time, so they are a good buy for a studio.

Table Top Easels

Aluminium   **Wooden**

Portable Sketching Easels

Lightweight metal easel

Sketching easel with paintbox

Portable sketching stool

BASIC TECHNIQUES

It's impossible to list all the special qualities of watercolour, or to itemize the ways in which paint will react in certain circumstances. It has an unpredictable character unlike any other medium — one of the reasons watercolour is often irritating and frustrating, but never boring.
There are half a dozen basic watercolour techniques, and an understanding and experience of them will give you the confidence to go on and exploit all the possibilities of watercolour on paper.

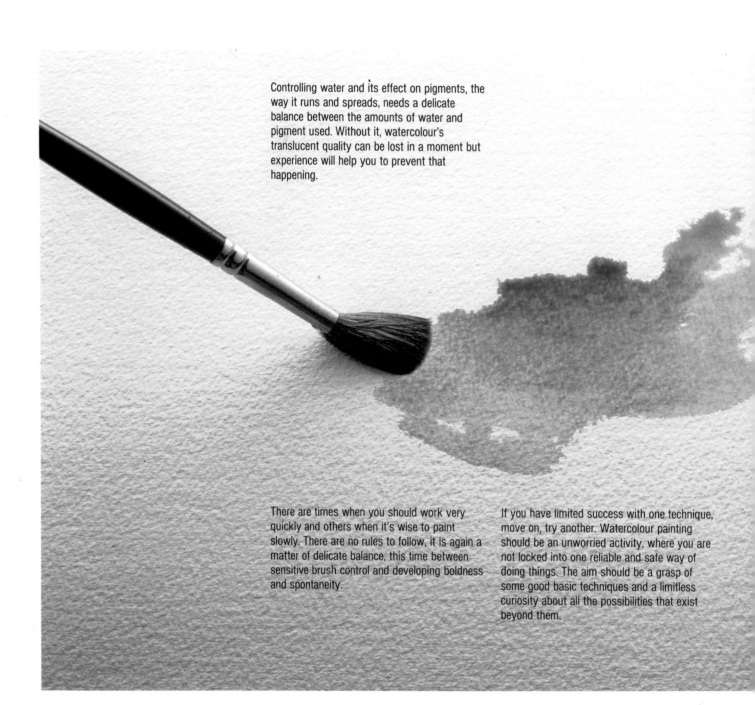

Controlling water and its effect on pigments, the way it runs and spreads, needs a delicate balance between the amounts of water and pigment used. Without it, watercolour's translucent quality can be lost in a moment but experience will help you to prevent that happening.

There are times when you should work very quickly and others when it's wise to paint slowly. There are no rules to follow, it is again a matter of delicate balance, this time between sensitive brush control and developing boldness and spontaneity.

If you have limited success with one technique, move on, try another. Watercolour painting should be an unworried activity, where you are not locked into one reliable and safe way of doing things. The aim should be a grasp of some good basic techniques and a limitless curiosity about all the possibilities that exist beyond them.

The most common anxiety among beginners is how to control the paint. Practise washing the paint onto your paper in even strips, to get the feel of the paint and what it will do on the paper. Add more and more clean water to your palette for each successive stroke to see how the colour changes and the effects created by the surface of the paper showing through.

Preliminary preparations

It may sound obvious, but it is essential to organize your work area. The materials should be close at hand with everything you need arranged on a flat surface. You will need something to mix colours on; for the early exercises, where a lot of pigment will be required for washes, shallow bowls or deep saucers might be suitable.

The quality of the watercolour paper you use for your early experiments is important. Smooth papers create less vibrant colours than rough papers and varying the dampness of the paper also affects watercolour. It's a good idea to start with stretching a sheet of 90lb Not/Cold Pressed watercolour paper. Even for early exercises I advise the use of purpose-made watercolour papers and not cartridge/drawing paper. 90lb Not/Cold Pressed paper gives excellent results but is not so expensive that it makes you hesitant to use for fear of spoiling it.

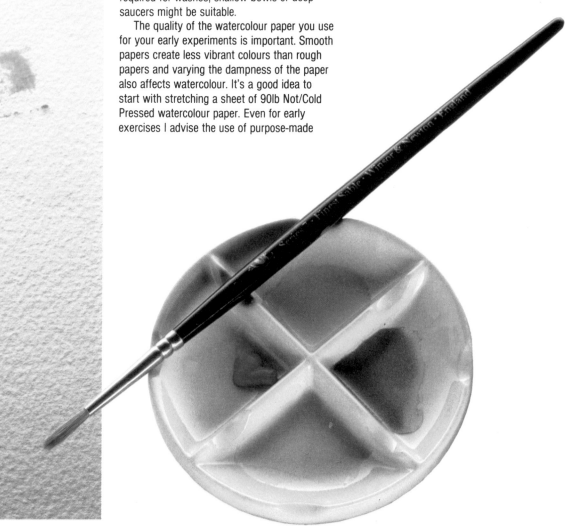

LAYING WASHES

The first basic technique of watercolour painting is the flat wash. This method is used constantly and it's a great help to the beginner to be able to lay a flat wash with confidence. It's purpose is to cover large areas which cannot be done with one brush stroke. Practise laying a wash and you are plunged into painting with watercolours.

Laying a Flat Wash

To begin, do not attempt to experiment on too large an area of paper. If you have stretched a half Imperial piece of paper, use half the area for the first wash.

Choose any colour you wish. Mix plenty of diluted colour in a deep saucer or bowl, preparing more than you think you will need. To maintain a consistent tone, you don't want to run out of colour half way through.

There are two types of flat wash, colour applied to either a wet or dry surface. It's slightly easier to lay a wash on a damp surface but you need to work quickly.

It's always daunting to approach a blank sheet of paper but the first stage in laying a wash is to dampen the paper with clean water. This helps you over that initial hurdle. It's difficult to spoil watercolour paper just with clean water and yet you feel you have committed yourself and have started to paint.

To lay a flat wash, first dampen the stretched paper carefully and then mix plenty of your chosen colour. Load a large flat brush with paint and take it across the paper in one stroke. Load the brush again and work back in the opposite direction, picking up the excess water from the previous line. Continue until the whole area is covered.

Dampening the paper should be done with care. If you damage the surface, a later application of watercolour will show any scratches or blemishes you have made. Use a clean sponge and clear water, or a soft, broad, house-painting brush, 37mm to 50mm (1½–2ins). Avoid making the paper too wet or it will buckle and could pull away from the board. The dampness of the paper will help to spread the colour evenly across it.

The drawing board should be tilted slightly, perhaps resting on a few books. This will help the wash to run down very gradually.

Take the largest flat soft brush you have, say the large oxhair. Too big a brush will be cumbersome to handle, a small one will be inadequate. Load the brush with the ready-mixed colour. Try to paint a continuous flat wash across the top of the damp paper, using one stroke. If it isn't perfect, don't go back and retouch it. Using more colour and working quickly, add a second line below the first, just picking up the stream of colour that has collected at the base of the first line. Working backwards and forwards, keep adding lines of colour until you reach the bottom.

Wet on wet — slow brush stroke

Wet on wet — swift brush stroke

The colour will diffuse and spread and gravity enables the paint to merge one line with another. The wash should be flat, transparent and consistent in tone and colour. The paper should be left to dry in the same position that you have painted it. If it is moved, the colour could run back up the paper and create an interesting but unwanted uneven wash.

Dry Surface Wash

This is simply colour applied to dry watercolour paper. Again, it's advisable to mix up beforehand more than enough diluted colour. Load the brush and draw it across the top of the dry paper, in just the same way as the wet surface wash. Continue down the paper, working from side to side. Don't go back to retouch. Try not to worry about "runs". The board will be at a slight angle and the colour should dry evenly. A dry surface does, however, collect the pigment on the texture of the watercolour paper. It dries, giving a dark and, varying with the weight and texture of the paper, broken wash, and the classic watercolour edge.

Wet on dry — slow brush stroke

Wet on dry — swift brush stroke

Graduated Washes

Just as you can employ two methods, wet and dry, to produce a flat wash, you can do the same with a graduated wash. It starts with strong and barely diluted colour at the top and steadily progresses down the paper, decreasing in tone as more water is added to the pigment, until it becomes so pale it merges into the white paper at the bottom. It's a method which is very useful for the early stages of background and skies.

You will need two jars of water, and plenty of ready-mixed colour in a bowl. Remember, in this exercise the colour will be intense at the start, so limit the amount of water to begin with. Using clear water, dampen the area to be painted. Rest the drawing board on a table. The board should be slightly tilted, at about 30°. If you have applied too much water, and it's lying in pools, blot it gently.

Load a large flat brush with the colour you have prepared and lay a band of colour across the top of the page. Don't hesitate. Quickly dip the brush into clean water, and run the brush under the first line of colour, picking up the paint which has run down to the base of the top line. Repeat this process. Each succeeding brush stroke will get weaker by adding increasing amounts of water and the wash will get paler as it reaches the bottom of the paper. This is a good example of the delicate balance of pigment and water. Leave the drawing board in the same position to dry. Don't touch it.

For the dry method, start by laying a brushstroke of strong colour along the top edge of a dry piece of stretched watercolour paper. Add clear water to your paint mixture and stir well. Lay a second diluted line of colour under the first, just picking it up. Continue down the paper, adding lines of increasingly diluted paint. The bottom line should be very thin paint indeed, mostly clear water. Leave the drawing board and paper in position to dry.

Wet on wet graduated wash

Wet on dry graduated wash

Variegated washes

Variegated washes are always fun to do because they are so unpredictable. You need three colours, a medium-size round sable brush and some stretched paper. For the first experiments you need not use large areas of paper. You could divide a medium-size piece of paper equally into two. Taking a sponge, and some clear water,

Two colours merging

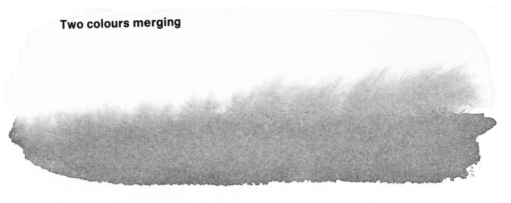

dampen the first area. The drawing board can lie horizontally on a table.

Choose a colour, paint a strip of colour onto the damp paper and wash the brush. Take a second colour and quickly lay a brush stroke next to the first. Repeat this process with a third colour. The edges of the colours will blend into each other.

As you will discover, the different ways variegated washes blend and react are endless and never the same. Try putting a thin colour down in a meandering way, in no particular direction. While it's still damp, place a little of a second colour on top. The colours will run together. Mix a thicker third colour and place a few brush strokes on the previously painted area and allow to dry.

Another technique is to dampen an area of stretched watercolour paper with clear water and paint over most of it, leaving a few white spaces. You will notice that because it's damp, you have to leave more white space than needed, as the colour will spread and join up. Working quickly, take a second colour and place it on the white spaces that have been left. Mix a little thicker third colour, painting into parts of the previous colours.

Wet into Wet

Wet into wet, as the title implies, means wet paint on a wet surface and the principle is very similar to that used in variegated washes. You paint not just on damp paper but onto wet paint that has already been applied. Wet into wet techniques typify a lot of watercolour painting, being unpredictable and risky. At times, you have to make snap decisions and work quickly.

FURTHER TECHNIQUES

You now understand several, good, basic watercolour techniques. They are honest, straightforward methods of painting and constant use of them will inevitably give you the confidence to create and produce original work. Beyond them, there are further techniques which, used too often and unthinkingly, could be called "tricks of the trade" and lead to bad habits and flashy superficialities. However, treated thoughtfully, special effects can be interesting, providing their use never intrudes on your own genuine reaction to a given subject and the truth of your own vision.

If additional techniques help you to use paint, water and paper more effectively and more creatively, that's fine. But if, at the end, your painting is only a catalogue of pictorial tricks, the result will be derivative and the interest somewhat limited.

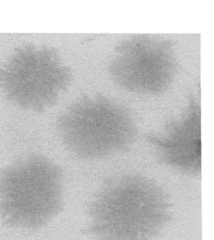

Starbursts
Lay a wash of colour and while the paint is still wet, drop in blobs of a second colour. The resulting mixture will create soft starburst effects.

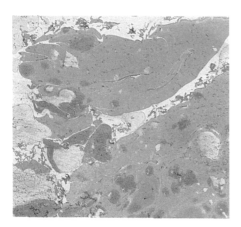

Dry Brush
As the name implies, you use a fairly dry brush and squeeze most of the colour out of the brush after you have picked up the pigment. It's a useful method when you are completing a picture, adding detail and texture.

Marbling (left)
Two colours intermingled on a dampened surface.

Scumbling (left)
This method can equally be called scrubbing. Take a fairly dry brush loaded with colour. Flattening the brush, and working in a circular movement, apply the pigment. The texture of watercolour paper will show through the paint.

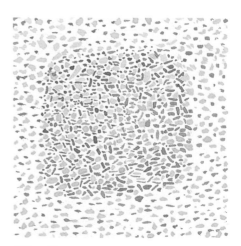

Stippling
This method of painting watercolours was sometimes used by the French Impressionists. Dots of different colours are laid side by side on white paper, using the tip of a fine sable. It is a boring method of working in watercolours if it is used to cover the whole surface, but it is interesting if used for textured contrast to larger areas of bold washes. Stippling can produce a rather stilted effect and the technique doesn't have the exciting, unpredictable quality that is associated with watercolour.

Valid use of unorthodox methods is fun and demonstrates the unending potential of watercolour materials. It's good working practice to collect anything you think might be used to make watercolour marks on paper. The following list of useful things to have by you in the studio, and the effects to be gained by them will, I hope, give you an appetite to try them all and experiment.

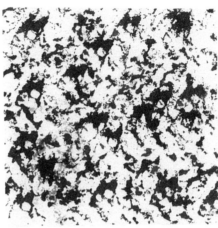

Sponges (left)

If you use a sponge for applying paint, it would be advisable not to use the one reserved for dampening paper; this must be kept clean. So purchase a small sponge for painting. Without using very much water, soak the sponge in paint and dab the sponge onto the paper. It produces broken, very unpredictable marks. Using more water in the sponge, you will be able to sweep it over large areas of paper.

It's not a method which produces sensitive, thoughtful painting, but it has its uses. I resort to the sponge and water when, for whatever reason, the painting I am doing appears to be going very wrong. (The reasons are usually overworking, which isn't difficult with watercolour, or over-attention to useless detail.) Having come to the reluctant conclusion that the painting isn't going well, I soak a sponge and use it for softening either the whole or parts of the painting. The washed-out and softer look of the painting, as a result of the sponging, usually encourages me to continue.

Paper Tissues

Blotting paint with a tissue eliminates brush marks and soaks up surplus water. As already mentioned, I use white toilet paper for blotting, cleaning and smearing paint. The rolls are inexpensive, disposable and much better than a paint rag. Kitchen roll is also useful for its distinctive bumpy texture which, like the sponge, can produce interesting irregular marks on the paper. If paper tissues become too wet particles may roll up and adhere to the surface of the painting. Leave them to dry before you brush them off.

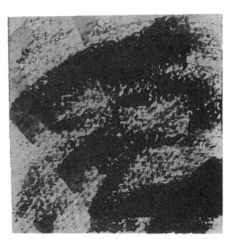

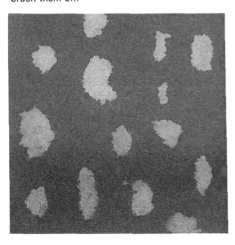

Razors (above)

Paint applied to the paper with a one-sided razor blade can create interesting flat-edged shapes. Keep the blade flat so that it doesn't dig in.

Cotton Buds (left)

A bud can be dipped into clean water and rubbed on dry paint to lift it. This is useful for revealing the white paper under a previously painted area.

Palette Knife

This is a very useful studio tool and can be used for applying paint. The fine edge can produce thin, sharp lines of paint on the paper, and the flat side spreads paint. It's also handy for easing paper off a watercolour block.

Masking Film or Paper Masks (left)

Sheets of transparent masking film are stocked by graphic art suppliers. The adhesive film can be peeled away from its backing sheet and laid onto the area of the painting which needs to be masked and protected. Unlike masking tape, it's a very accurate method. The mask is cut out using a scalpel or craft knife.

Its advantages are that, unlike tape or fluid masks, its transparency makes it possible to see what is underneath the mask while you are painting all around it. The big drawback is that if you are using stretched watercolour paper, it's very easy to cut through not only the mask of transparent film, but into the watercolour paper as well, producing something resembling a jigsaw puzzle.

In contrast to masking film, which leaves a hard edge, a loose, paper mask will allow paint to seep under the edge, which creates a softer effect, particularly if the paper has a torn edge. Hold the paper mask down on the paper with one hand, while you paint with the other.

Masking Tape

A roll of masking tape is very useful in the studio as it is a quick and convenient way of masking out areas of paper while you are painting. It is a method best used when accuracy isn't very important — for example, when parts of the painting are to be sprayed or splattered. When the paint has dried, the masking tape can be lifted and removed. Masking tape and fluids do not work very well on cheap paper or cartridge/drawing paper. They stick to it and tear the surface on removal. But it is a successful method on smooth or medium-weight watercolour papers. On rough, heavy paper, paint has a tendency to creep under the masking tape and invade areas where it's not required.

Masking Fluid

Bottles of masking fluid, which has a creamy look and texture, can be purchased at most art suppliers. Shake the bottle to ensure a thick enough consistency. If the fluid is too thin it won't resist paint.

Masking fluid can be used to preserve those areas of the painting which you wish to keep white. Don't apply the fluid till the original paint is dry or it will run. Similarly, let the application dry throughly before you work over it.

If you need to recover the areas masked with the fluid, it's very easy to remove with the end of a clean finger or an eraser, providing the paint is dry. It it's not dry, you will only succeed in smearing the paint.

Wax resist

This method is easily achieved by rubbing an ordinary wax candle over the surface of a piece of paper. Wherever the candle has touched the paper the wax deposit will resist the watercolour.

Sandpaper

In desperation, I have resorted to sanding down paintings with varying degrees of success. Sanding softens and breaks up the surface but it is tricky. Attempt this method only if you really feel that you cannot rescue the painting in any other way.

Scratching and scraping

Using the wooden end of a brush, scratch into a layer of wet paint, which has just been painted over a previous colour that has dried. You need to use quick and vigorous movements. Using a plastic comb can achieve the same sort of result. The use of a razor blade or the side of a craft knife blade on watercolour paper has to be done with thought and care. It is one method of reducing the tone of a painted area, but it can destroy the surface of the paper, making it difficult, or sometimes impossible, to work on afterwards. It is useful for scraping out highlights when the painting is nearly finished.

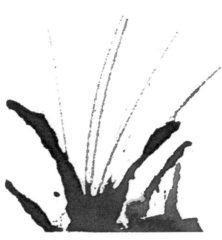

Drinking Straws

Using drinking straws, blobs of watercolour can be blown and spread in different directions. However, this is another haphazard, and very unpredictable, watercolour method, to be used with discretion.

Hair dryer

A hair dryer can be used to speed the drying process of a painting, but be careful. The force of the warm air can move wet paint very quickly in a direction that you did not intend.

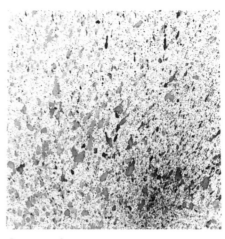

Splattering

Coat the top of a toothbrush with pigment, hold it over a sheet of paper and run a finger or a knife over the bristles. The paint will splatter and spray onto the paper. It's a very haphazard method but your aim will improve with practice. It might be prudent to surround the area with newspaper to prevent over-splatter.

String

Soak lengths of string in the paint and then drag them across the paper. The texture of the string creates a pretty, broken line on the paper, which is difficult to create with a brush.

Household washing-up liquid

Adding washing-up liquid to pigment produces, not surprisingly, a bubbly texture. But be warned: if too much of the liquid is added, the paint never dries.

Baby oil

Put a few drops of baby oil into a small water pot, swirl the brush around in this before dipping it in the paint. The oil acts as a resistor to the paint but is less resistant than candlewax or masking fluid and so more of the colour remains on the paper.

Putty/kneadable rubber

This shouldn't be treated as a common practice. Its use will reduce the tone and intensity of an area of colour, but too much use has a deadening effect on dry watercolour paint.

SUBJECTS
AND STYLES

This section suggests ways of approaching and looking at subjects, noting their details and what to look for when painting them. The most important steps to take before you start painting are explained here, such as choosing a subject, deciding how to convey what first attracted you to it; then, how to arrange it, and the importance of sketching and drawing as a means of note-taking.

The selection of finished paintings as well as the step-by-step sequences show you ways of painting landscapes, seascapes, water, flowers, people, buildings and animals, and the problems and methods of painting each one are discussed.

In the end it is your own vision and method of working that are important. Here you are encouraged to explore and enjoy watercolour painting, and to develop a style of your own.

APPROACHING THE SUBJECT

There are many ways to approach a watercolour painting. Yours will vary, too,
depending on how you look at each subject. It's no good waiting for inspiration:
plunge right in. The end result will reflect your enjoyment.
What to paint, and how to go about it, are the first questions beginners ask. There
is hardly anything which isn't paintable. The choice is unlimited, but things you
like and know well are good subjects to start with.

Looking at subject matter

A sincere interest in and curiosity about the
possible subject matter will help you to
understand it and paint it well. It isn't necessary
to travel miles to gather inspiration — a good
painting can be of something quite insignificant.
The most spectacular scenes do not always
make good subjects for painting. We are
surrounded by visually interesting subjects;
observe how your world really looks.

Above: Jacqueline Rizvi's sensitive
painting of a Chinese bowl shows
her love for this kind of subject, its
simplicity and purity. Her first
consideration is where the cup
should be in the picture space.
Perfect placing is of the greatest
importance. And, the table surface
is considered to be just as
important as the painting of the
cup. This painting demonstrates
how a very simple object can
provide fascinating subject material.

Left: Pamela Kay chooses to paint
the most commonplace objects and
says, "Until you draw these familiar
everyday objects, you don't realise
how beautiful they are." Most
people overlook humble objects
because they are familiar, and it's
only when they are explored in
terms of paint and colour that their
simple beauty is revealed.

Left: Jacqueline Rizvi's bedroom with a small chair in a corner of the artist's bedroom. She first noticed the possibilities of painting the chair while doing the housework. She hadn't realised it would be worth painting before. A subject so simple depends largely upon perspective and subtle tone modulation. In both

Anne Maclaren's painting (below) of books and objects and also in Lucy Willis' picture (bottom) of a hat and cushions, these paintings work because the artists have employed acute observation and are very sensitive to the possibilities around them.

What to paint

As you read this, look up. Look in front of you. Now consider the possibility of painting whatever there is in front of you. It could be the cluttered kitchen table, a bedroom lamp or a flower border in the garden. It doesn't matter. Good subject matter is all around us: fascinating objects, colour combinations, interesting effects of light and shadow.

Don't waste time arranging objects to paint; the result will probably be self-conscious and contrived. There are numerous half-hidden subjects tucked away in corners of greenhouses and under hedgerows. Small, intimate still-life subject matter can be found everywhere.

A natural connection between the subjects for a still-life is always a good idea. It could be a colour connection or simply that they belong together: things found in the kitchen — food and utensils; in the bedroom — discarded clothes; or in the greenhouse — flowerpots and garden tools. This type of natural grouping of subject matter is ideal for your early paintings.

Having selected your subject, you now need to choose the viewpoint from which you will paint it. It may be that looking at your subject at close range will suit your purposes, or that a viewpoint from farther back will enable you to include an interesting background. Looking through a door or window at your subject will literally give you a framework within which you can work.

At this stage, a few pencil studies will help

you to investigate all the possibilities. Many artists first draw in the main ingredients with pencil. Your drawing does not need to be an elaborate or detailed one, but be as accurate as you can. Quite often when people start to draw, they tend to draw what they think things look like, rather than how an object really is. So don't start with preconceived ideas about the appearance of anything. Try looking at it as if you have never seen it before.

Explore, too, the relationship between the objects you are going to draw and paint; not only the objects themselves but the shapes and the spaces between them. The effects of light, sharp edges and diffused areas should all be observed and noted.

Your foundation drawing should be accurate without being overworked. Your watercolour shouldn't be a colouring-in exercise, but rather a natural progression from the original drawing.

45

Drawing

Drawing is an essential part of any kind of painting: it helps you to search for detail, it is part of the creative process in watercolour painting.

Drawing has several functions: as a preparatory study, or an on-the-spot note, or just as a guideline, before colour and pigment are used on a painting.

How much drawing you do before starting to paint is a matter of choice. Experience will teach you just how much you need to do before you start to paint. Using a sketch book constantly to make notes of compositions and ideas for paintings is invaluable and very good working practice.

Although it makes sense to do small sketches beforehand to establish the composition of the painting, the danger lies in taking these sketches too far, spending so much time working them out that all your creative effort has gone into the sketch and nothing is left to say with colour and brush.

Above and right: these pages from Albany Wiseman's sketch book show that you can record situations simply, in pencil, drawing on a single page or across the whole spread of the open sketch book. There is enough information in these drawings to form the basis for paintings to be completed back in the studio.

Left: Albany Wiseman's drawing of an avenue with trees was drawn in France and later "squared up", to enable the artist to enlarge the drawing onto watercolour paper back in the studio. This was done by drawing a corresponding number of squares in a larger size on a new sheet of paper. The squares were then numbered and the image that appeared in each square of the original sketch was drawn in on its equivalent square on the new paper.

Below: There is a delightful feeling of spring and fresh air in this sketch by Albany Wiseman drawn near an open air café, situated in a park.

Many artists draw everything in pencil first; the result is that the subsequent watercolour becomes a colouring-in exercise. The opposite way is to draw directly with a brush, in watercolour, without a preliminary drawing. The painting is then allowed to develop and grow. The first sketch marks are light and gradually the forms become defined, or perhaps the first marks are altered and moved, but the whole picture is developed in watercolour from the start. The mistakes, and the painter's thoughts are there as part of the painting.

Sketch Books

Drawing constantly is a very good way to improve your fluency as a watercolourist. It is the foundation of all forms of painting, so try to draw every day. A sketch book is ideal for this purpose.

Most professional artists keep and use sketch books, and it's a matter of choice whether they use a large sketch book, or one that fits into a pocket. Sketching is a good habit to acquire and the main benefit is that by constantly looking for things to draw and sketching them, you train your eyes to look and "see" all the time.

Draw directly from life: objects, scenes or people in the house, everyday things. A sketch book can be used almost as a diary. Use each page fully, and try to put in as much information as you can before turning to a new page.

A small sketch book can be held without too many people noticing that you are drawing and possibly becoming self-conscious. A lot of notes and small sketches could be the basis for later watercolours, and notes on colours are particularly useful. The sketch can be covered in colour notes and any other information you may need later. Record and make a note of anything that interests you. There is very little you cannot draw and paint.

Time and circumstances will dictate just how much detail you can put in. The act of attempting to put something down on paper will make you far more observant and visually aware. A sketch book will build up your confidence, for it is a private book in which you can try to draw or paint anything, and not be afraid of making mistakes.

Most sketch book paper isn't suitable for watercolour. So, if you are sketching with watercolours, use as little as possible.

Taking photographs is a useful addition to sketching, both as reference and as a reminder. But photographs cannot express that moment of visual excitement that attracted you in the first place. Drawings in sketch books, however, can and are therefore a never-ending source of subject matter for the basis of future paintings.

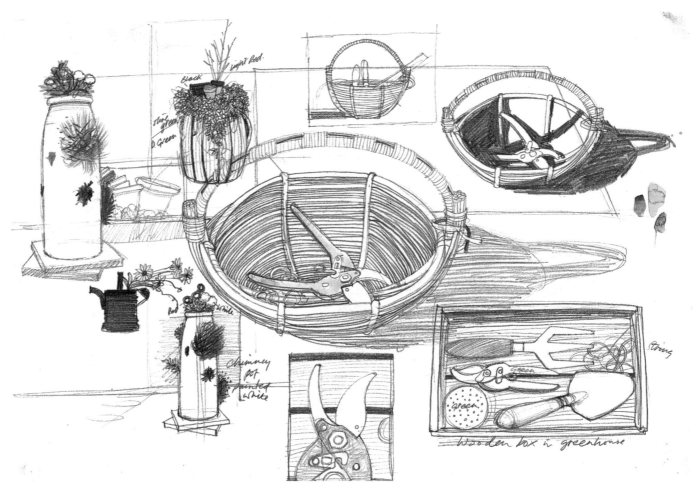

Shape and format

One of the purposes of drawing a rough sketch before you start a watercolour is to plan the content and the shape of the painting.

A little thought beforehand will usually prevent such obvious problems as trying to fit a painting of a tall tree into a horizontal, thin rectangle. A successful arrangement is usually arrived at by trial and error. Try out a series of different groupings of the main elements that you want to include in your painting. After a time you will find you develop a "feel" for a good composition.

You can start your painting in the middle of a large sheet of paper and then wait to see how its shape and form develop as you paint. You can even cut pieces off when it is finished. The shape and size of your painting can, within reason, be anything you wish. But you should remember that some shapes are more suitable for certain subjects and compositions than other shapes.

Sketches serve as a good reminder of shapes and colours. You can always re-arrange the elements later, in your painting, as I did for the box of gardening tools, **above**.

The edges of the box formed a natural framework for the painting, but I re-arranged the tools to fully explore the relationship between their shapes, colours and textures.

At the start it can be useful to paint within the standard rectangle; this encourages anyone looking at the painting to use their eyes and to take a progressive interest in one part of the picture after another in a relaxed way.

A horizontal, elongated shape has the effect of making the eye flit from left to right and back again. A square shape has to be treated with caution; the main point of interest needs to be positioned very carefully, as the corners of the painting take on a very real importance. Lastly, an upright rectangle can be used to emphasize vertical elements in the painting. So, experiment with all these shapes.

From the same series of sketches, I borrowed two drawings of the basket. In one I had recorded the detail of the basket and its contents; in the other I came up with a very satisfying composition in which I have placed the basket off-centre but have used the shadow to balance the overall image.

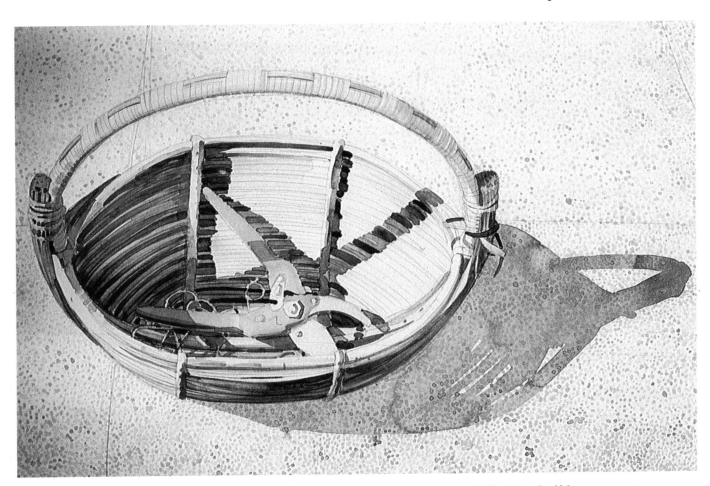

Using a viewfinder

It helps to "see" and compose a painting by using a rectangular cardboard "window" to look at a likely subject. It isolates the subject, by framing off the background. You can improvise a viewfinder by arranging your hands and fingers into a rectangular shape.

The cardboard viewfinder consists of a larger version of a photographic slide holder. Simply cut a rectangle in the middle of a firm piece of cardboard — 75 × 50mm (3 × 1in) should be large enough.

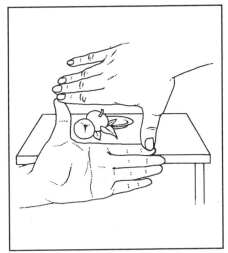

What to do if it goes wrong

Painting is not a very logical business. Unfortunately progressive stages do not always work and even professional artists never know whether the pigment and water are doing what they want them to. A watercolour can and often does go badly wrong. But this element of chance makes painting more exciting and apparent disasters can very often be retrieved.

When a watercolour becomes dull and overworked, even "muddy", sponge it out. The softening result may well be an improvement. Alternatively, rubbing it down, when it is dry, with sandpaper, will allow you to rework the painting.

Setting up a Still-life

It is worthwhile establishing a few basic guidelines when you arrange a still-life to paint. Interest in and a genuine liking for the objects that you have chosen is important. You could be inspired by the texture, the colour or just the way light falls on a simple object. Very ordinary, plain things often prove to be very suitable for painting.

Wander around your house and garden making a mental note of things that appeal to you; you might like to make a collection of potential still-life objects as you go along. Sometimes, when you have space, it is fun to collect objects of a similar colour from which to select and create groups for a painting later on.

Place your collection of objects on a table or on a shelf. It's an idea to place them in an upright cardboard box not only to protect them from the children or the cat but also to contain them and provide a framework for your painting.

The position and arrangement of the objects that you are going to paint can take as little or as much time as you wish. The variations are endless, but too many roughs end in confusion, and too little thought beforehand can be regretted after hours of painting.

The first decision made by the artist here was that this still-life should be contained within the confined area of a cardboard box. In the first drawing (**above**) the box was placed upright with two jugs arranged inside it and three apples in front of it. Strong lighting from the left produced interesting shadows.

In the second rough (**left**) the box was placed horizontally. The two tall jugs were replaced by a jar and a bowl which fit into the vertical depth better, and another apple was added. The lighting was altered slightly so that the inside of the box was almost completely in shadow.

Try out several arrangements or groupings sketching each one to see how it works until you find a satisfactory still-life. Draw in the basic shapes but avoid putting in too much detail because you will dissipate your energy and interest before you even lift a paintbrush!

Now, paint quickly. Complete the watercolour in one session, and you will look forward to painting your next still-life.

It was felt at this stage that the box should be positioned once more in an upright position (**above**). A jar with a large cork was placed in the righthand side of the box, and the apples in front of the box, one slightly behind the other two. The space between the apples is important; the position and colour of the apple on the righthand side creates a useful "full-stop" to the painting.

With the box in a horizontal position (**above**) the bowl was replaced with a casserole dish and one of the apples was removed. The lighting was also altered so that both the interior of the box and the objects were clearly visible. The empty righthand corner of the box could have been a problem, assuming too much importance, but it was decided to leave it as it was. The small, well-lit handle in the centre of the still-life created a sharp point of interest among the diffused shadows and hard and soft edges of the other objects.

By changing the lighting so that it just caught the edges of the objects but left the interior of the box dark, the handle of the casserole was no longer important (**below**).

STILL-LIFE IN A CARDBOARD BOX

Annie Williams

After drawing several roughs and sketches, one arrangement is chosen and the still-life is drawn lightly with an HB pencil on 250lb Bockingford paper. This is a very good watercolour paper to manipulate paint on, and also it has the advantage of being thick and heavy enough not to need stretching. A simple outline drawing is made at this stage — the position and proportions of the objects are the important factors, not the detail.

Above: a light wash of raw umber is brushed over the outside edges and the inside of the box and allowed to dry before a wash of ultramarine and alizarin and a little cerulean and raw umber is placed behind the objects, creating a dark background.

Left: when the first stage has dried, additional washes of raw Sienna and Payne's grey are laid on the inside edges of the box to give some feeling of depth. A light wash of colour is brushed onto the pots to get a better idea of how the painting will look, and to soften the rather severe edges.

Far left: the paint is fairly wet at this stage and additional colours can be dropped into the wet areas to achieve the effect required. The apples are now painted with a diluted wash of cadmium yellow and while it's still wet, a very light touch of cadmium red is placed on the righthand side and allowed to spread.

Left: additional light washes are added to give form to both the objects in the box and to the apples, without attempting to include too much detail.

Above: in the final picture the area behind the pots is darkened and then hastily blotted. This throws the objects into relief, making the image more three-dimensional.

LANDSCAPES

A landscape doesn't have to be made up of green fields, hills and trees. Urban landscapes are often more familiar and offer just as many interesting opportunities for picture making. Every landscape has a character of its own which you can paint, though it changes constantly because of the time of day and weather conditions. This can provide endless fascinating subject matter, but it can also give the watercolour painter a series of painting challenges. Expressing space and perspective are the most obvious ones but the changing effects of colour, texture and light can also present difficulties.

Space and Distance

One of the main requirements in a landscape is to give an impression of space and distance. There are simple methods of painting space convincingly. Simplified tones and colours separated into the foreground and the middle and far distance can help to explain space and distance and the planes which make up a landscape. Colours can be used in a systematic way to convey depth in a painting, and understanding how different sorts of pigments behave, either mixed together or placed side by side, will enable you to paint more skilfully. Ideas on colour are important, but at an early stage of an artist's development they can be inhibiting and prevent the more important activity of close and accurate observation.

Above: in your first landscape paintings just respond to the landscape and adopt simple straightforward methods. For example, in the foreground use warm colours, such as reds and browns, which generally advance optically. In the middle ground and on the horizon use cooler colours — greens and blues – which recede.

Left: in this painting the artist has conveyed a receding landscape by painting the foreground in a dark tone and progressing through a middle tone to a light one on the horizon.

Left: Another basic technique that you can use to create a sense of distance between the objects in the painting is to paint the foreground with crisp definition and the background with hazy lines and colours. Perhaps you could use a drier paint in the foreground than in the middle and far distance. To produce a diffuse effect in the background use a "wet in wet" technique, dropping very diluted pigment onto wet colour on the paper.

Time

When you are considering painting a landscape, ask yourself: How much time do I have? What can I achieve in that period of time? The answers to these basic questions will affect the size and scope of your work. A scene will look very different in the early morning from later in the afternoon and will have changed yet again by evening. This fact limits the time that you can spend painting, which in turn influences the size of the picture. If you worked on one painting from early morning to late at night, you would experience so many changes in light and shadow that there would probably be at least six different impressions of the scene in one painting. The result — interesting confusion, and frustration for the artist. With constantly changing light it is best to decide what it is that attracted you to the scene. Make a few pencil sketches to clarify your ideas and to establish the correct proportions and main features that you want to include, and then quickly and simply put down your impression before it fades and disappears. If you change your mind, then start the painting again.

Landscape "Markers"

An often-used method of establishing depth and distance in a landscape is to use a familiar object in the foreground which, because of its familiarity, immediately provides a guide to size and distance. A tree in the foreground, a house in the middle distance, and mountains in the background (**right**) all combine to explain the distance and space between them in a mechanical and predictable way.

Below: A recognizable shape, such as a farm building, drawn in perspective, immediately creates a sense of depth and distance.

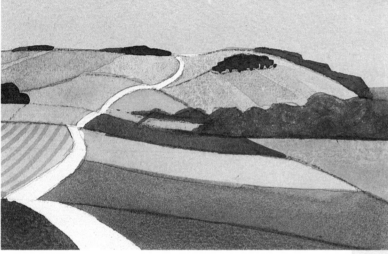

Above: A road which crosses hills and valleys and recedes into the distance can help to describe the contours and depth of a landscape.

Below: A very simple device is to use linear perspective aided by parallel converging lines as in an avenue of trees. The decreasing size of the trees implies distance.

Right: Try painting a landscape that has as its main point of interest a foreground feature such as a stone wall and gate. The gate gives a visual "marker" from which the eye can travel to distant parts of the painting. (The size of the cottage relates to the size of the gate and implies its distance from it.) The position of such a feature is helpful; it establishes the order of things.

Strong sunlight

Light plays a vital part in creating mood and atmosphere. The clarity of the light in southern Europe produces totally different effects from the wet, atmospheric, soft light in northern Europe. Colours appear to be more intense in the south. Walk around the streets of Greece or the South of France and you will find that there is almost too much to draw and paint: decorative balconies, blinds and shutters are everywhere, as are dramatic shadows and patterns created by the intense light. Experiment in sketches and with watercolour on how you can capture these effects.

Landscape and the Colour Green

Avoid preconceived ideas about the colour of a landscape. Often it appears to be totally green, but green must be handled with care — it can be a coarse and insensitive colour. Spend a little time looking hard at your subject; make a note of the yellows, browns, greys and blues that can be found in a landscape. Don't use the same green for everything, it becomes boring and very uninteresting. Use colour to explain space and distance visually, using mixtures of both warm and cool colours to describe the space, depth and character of a landscape.

Above: There are qualities found in landscapes which should be exploited by the watercolour painter: rough and smooth textures; linear qualities; hard-edged objects, fuzzy, soft and out-of-focus areas.

FARMHOUSE IN THE ARDÈCHE

Juliette Palmer

Ideally, Juliette Palmer sits in the open to draw with the board across her knees to support paper and materials. In a comfortable temperature and consistent light, she will work on the same subject for two or more days observing and drawing carefully. If time or the weather prevent leisurely work on the spot, she makes colour notes. Rather than paint a quick interpretation in watercolour, she prefers to draw with coloured pencils and sometimes wax or oil crayons for speed and easy handling.

After drawing in the outlines, the process of applying colour begins. Juliette uses Hollingsworth Kent rough paper or a Saunders NOT/ Cold Pressed surface. She prefers a rounded point on her brushes to produce blobs of colour. So she often cuts the tips off new brushes to get the effect she requires.

The shapes of the rocks, bushes and trees are explored with the brush. It is used to define the area of colour and also to isolate the white and pale areas which will be left as unpainted white paper or as very light washes.

The artist moves from area to area on the painting, working up to and around features in the landscape. By painting the areas and spaces between objects she discovers interesting and unpredictable shapes.

Her method of working, isn't predictable. She is always surprised by what arrives and says, "I want to see at the end a well-integrated painting composed of new delights and new achievements. Even with their limited scope I hope that my paintings will have my personal stamp born of personal invention."

Skies and Clouds

The sky should not be treated merely as a background, because its colour ultimately affects the landscape. The time of day, the direction of the sun, the way the clouds are moving and the weather conditions will affect the colour and appearance of the sky and consequently the colour and mood of the landscape.

Time spent studying the sky before you paint will pay dividends. Once you start painting, it's important to work quickly to capture the sky before it changes.

STORMY COAST

Polly Raynes

Stormy skies and clouds are difficult to study
and paint. Apart from it being a problem trying
to paint in stormy weather, the constantly
changing light and subtleties of colour and form
present any watercolour painter with a complex
challenge. The first facts to establish are the
source of light and the direction of the clouds.
Careful observation is absolutely necessary
before any successful painting can be
attempted. Heavy dark skies and dramatic
lighting have to be analysed and broken down
into logical painting stages from light to dark.
After deciding on a course of action you must
keep to this despite the changes in front of you.
If you do not, this will only lead to confusion
and irreparable mistakes.

Right: Polly Raynes drew in the
main areas of the painting with
speed and energy. The style and
atmosphere were immediately
established by the way these first
pencil marks were drawn.

Above: in keeping with the subject
matter, the artist decided to create
an impression of dampness and
softness in the sky and landscape.
The first washes of colour were
therefore freely painted with a
loaded brush and plenty of fresh
water. No attempt was made to
restrict the washes.

Left and below: the painting was kept in a state of constant change by maintaining its dampness as far as was possible. The painting was laid flat to ensure that the paint did not run down the surface but rather dried naturally in soft wet-against-wet patches. Polly Raynes took care not to overwork the storm clouds, and allowed this area to dry before additional darker brush strokes were laid on. If too much heavy colour had been applied too early, the effect would have been a mass of flat dark colour without any of the subtle tones that were needed here. It was only when the artist painted the rocks in the foreground that a small brush was used and details were drawn. Too much added detail would, in this case, only have lessened the impression of damp mist and rain.

WINTER LANDSCAPES

Albany Wiseman

A fall of snow transforms landscapes — the reflective quality of snow produces a bright light, despite a weak sun, the shadows are long, and trees assume a different, skeletal, shape. These changes give a familiar landscape a new excitement. Drawings made in the car or through a window will allow you to study and paint the effects of snow without freezing; these sketches and notes will be useful as a basis for a larger painting which can be completed back at home. There are also tricks and techniques, such as sprinkling salt onto the wet surface of watercolour which produces an effect that looks something like falling snow. However, as with any subject, techniques like this are best avoided or used with discretion. Not only will salt rot the paper but it means that you will have stopped looking hard at your subject. Paint what you see honestly. Using too many tricks will result in superficial painting, close observation and careful drawing will produce original work.

Above: using earlier drawings made in a sketchbook, Albany Wiseman pencilled in the main areas of the composition lightly, working on a 46 × 60cm (18 × 24in) Arches watercolour block, of semi-rough 140lb paper.

Above: "Working on a reasonably large area gives more scope for broad washes," observes Albany Wiseman. The first wash was of blue-grey (mixed from Antwerp blue, neutral tint, Payne's grey, and a touch of rose madder), using a large wash brush and a smaller pointed sable. (It was then dried with the aid of a hair dryer.) This was followed by a second broad wash, using Vandyke brown and neutral tint. Care was taken to avoid the areas of white paper which would be left completely unpainted throughout. The artist wanted to keep the brilliance of the white paper intact.

Above: the broad washes were allowed to dry thoroughly, and then masking fluid was applied to delineate the stonework on the buildings (see detail **left**). Again, this was completely dry before more colour was applied. Using a small pointed sable the artist drew and painted the details: windows, the branches of trees, and small areas of local colour. When he is painting broad areas Albany Wiseman mixes up more colour than he will probably need, and finds tubes preferable, because they are easier to mix in a large palette or saucer. The water is changed often so that it's always clean.

TREES

Painting trees is not dissimilar to painting human beings. It's surprisingly difficult. Trees are complex structures, they have an underlying structure, a skeleton, and drawing and painting them with masses of detail seems a daunting prospect. It's a good idea to draw trees at regular intervals throughout the year, but particularly in winter when it's easy to analyse their structure. An understanding of this will help you to paint trees convincingly when they are covered with a mass of summer foliage.

Spruce

Cypress

Zelkova

Pine

English elm

Amelanchier

Weeping Willow

Right: it will help you enormously if you make watercolour sketches of trees, however rough, to understand their growth and particular characteristics. Albany Wiseman's sketch was done in springtime in a village square in the South of France. Although the watercolour was done quickly the particular character of the trees was carefully observed and noted. The sketch also serves as a good reminder and reference for a larger scale painting. The trees make a delightful framework for the composition and direct the eye to the almost abstract qualities of the houses at the end of the square.

Left: draw and paint trees as often as possible without their leaves. As these examples show, trees vary in shape and structure.

Right: early one morning Jacqueline Rizvi, seeing that it had snowed overnight, decided to stop work on the painting she was doing and paint the snow and lime trees outside. She chose to work on a lilac-grey Fabriano Roma paper. This provided a suitable background tint and also added texture to the painting. While painting she noticed numerous colour changes in the tree trunk, which she incorporated. She found it useful to identify the main branches, some of which were light, and some dark. The spaces and shapes, between the branches were all carefully noted and painted. At the end of day she stopped painting as the snow had melted.

Left: in Charlotte Halliday's work the effects of winter sunlight and the blowing wind all come through in this beautifully observed painting. The scene is near the artist's house and the trees are drawn with delicacy and knowledge; each one has a character of its own. The end result is very powerful and convincing.

Below: sun and light play an important part in Reginald Dent's painting, shown here. Again the trees not only form an excellent framework for the composition but their linear qualities and the way they are painted also give a feeling of vigour and life.

Left: painting every leaf doesn't always work as it is rarely convincing. But in Juliette Palmer's painting it is, because she gives the general shape of the leaves rather than painting them in exact detail. The feeling given is that the artist sat on the hillside and looked very carefully at the structure of everything in the picture. By superimposing a mass of wild flowers on a mass of trees she has produced a real sense of growth and abundance.

THE GARDEN

Juliette Palmer

It's worth considering the hazards that can befall any artist before you set out to paint. These mainly involve the weather, but can also involve the curiosity of strangers and small children. There is also the annoyance of forgetting some vital piece of equipment or loading yourself down with too much clutter. At first, it is a good idea to work close to home; the surroundings may seem familiar, but spend time sketching and looking. Gardens, patios or backyards provide colour, tone, patterns and textures, and plenty of unexpected subject matter for watercolours.

As with so many of Juliette Palmer's studies, this drawing was made in a large sketch book. The style has as its base good observational drawing. There is an underlying understanding of perspective, a clear intention in shape and form and a certainty of outline. The style is linear and very informative with colour notes written in. It is a clear analysis of quite a complex subject.

The drawing was transferred onto stretched watercolour paper, and then painted with constant reference to the colour notes. This was done as soon as possible while her memory was fresh. "One tries to relive the total impression that one received as one works — the sounds, scents, movements — to produce atmosphere in the painting", she says. The work of placing the colour was done at random, wherever her interest led her, gradually covering the paper. Great care should be taken not to place colour where it's not required, because once covered, the white of the paper cannot be redeemed.

The work continued piecemeal, the paint always applied in a translucent diluted state, gradually becoming darker. The shapes of flowers and foliage are explored with the brush, which slowly defines the area and extent of the colour. The shapes and tones between flowers and their background are carefully considered and painted. Throughout the artist tries not to lose the immediacy of the medium. The end result is a cohesion and a distilled intensity.

SEASCAPES

The seaside is a great source of material and is forever changing. It could be a pattern and colour, the mood of the sea or the shapes of bathers, fishermen or boats that attract you. The surrounding landscape can vary from rocky cliffs to flat, sandy stretches of beach. Seaside architecture varies from dilapidated beach houses to new modern marinas. Sketches and notes made at the seaside can be rewarding for future work.

Because of the physical problems of painting outdoors and by the sea it is necessary to keep a flexible attitude and respond to constantly changing circumstances. Tides change, the rock you have chosen to sit on gradually becomes uninhabitable, boats and people move. Working on a small scale, simply and quickly produces a number of invaluable sketches and notes.

Careful observation pays dividends. You may choose to concentrate on individual areas of interest: a solitary boat, a lighthouse, sunbathers, the harbour wall or beach huts.

Watch the sea. Draw and understand, for example, how a wave breaks. Isolate and analyse the movement of the water. The translucent quality of water and its constantly changing appearance provide a challenge to any artist.

Above: Harry Eccleston's painting of the boats on the beach is not only a record of something seen but also has an abstract quality in the placing of the shapes and strips of colour. It has a wonderful feeling of sunlight and space.
Left: these tiny pencil studies of ships and boats by Harry Eccleston show the infinite variety of size and shape of passing and moored boats, any one of which might be used later in a finished painting.

Above, above right and right: the sketchbook studies of people on the beach done by Harry Eccleston provided a rich source of material for a series of paintings which were completed in the studio. Using just a pencil and a small sketchbook he could easily draw people while they sat or stood naturally. They were not embarrassed because he was able to draw them without their knowledge, which resulted in a series of charming drawings.

Left: the watercolour study of the beach hut and chairs was painted on a pre-stretched watercolour pad by the author. These pads of paper are an ideal alternative to a sketchbook for more detailed studies in colour, when time and circumstances permit. A simple, straightforward view was taken because the pattern of the lines and strips of colour were the qualities that he first noticed and, as work progressed, the importance of light and sunlight also became evident.

ON THE BEACH

Harry Eccleston

Harry Eccleston's main interest is the underlying abstract relationships in a subject. All his paintings are produced from sketches (**above**) or photographs. The finished work is planned and painted in the studio where such relationships can be controlled.

Having worked out how he feels the picture will be painted, he prepares a "master" tracing (**below**). Of course, the plan is never accurately followed. Every painting takes on a life of its own as work progresses, but it is in the tracing that Harry Eccleston aims to preserve the elements that attracted him in the first place. He will then transfer the tracing on to stretched watercolour paper, and refine it with a fine pencil. Using masking fluid he will "protect" certain features, such as the boats and the figures, from the large areas of wash.

Left: it's always a good idea to make as many sketches as possible of a subject you're interested in creating a "catalogue" from which you can later borrow shapes, colours and movements, for another painting.

Left: the sky and beach were built up with many pale washes. (Harry used a hair dryer to speed up the drying process.) The artist often uses more than twenty washes to achieve the effects needed. This enables one area to have great variety in tone and colour. By using many washes he could build up a "blue" from very many different blues.

As soon as the watercolour was completely dry, the masking fluid was carefully removed. Colour was then added to the areas that had been protected. Adjustments were made to the large areas of wash and the picture was gently balanced for both tone and colour (**below**). This, for Harry, is the exciting part. Wherever possible he does it with as much freedom as he can allow — for him he is not just painting a watercolour but rather painting *a picture* in watercolour.

WATER

Watercolour is an ideal and natural medium for painting water because its characteristics are so like those of water. Take a broad view of the stretch of water. Study its movement and ripples. Notice how the water, land and rocks meet, and how its reflections, colours and moods are always changing. Reflections play a vital part in explaining what is happening to the surface of the water, as well as echoing the solid forms above the surface. Weather and the conditions of the sky will also be reflected in the colour of the water. So, select an aspect that interests you, simplify it and then stay with the aims you have set for yourself.

Above and left: to the beginner, it may seem that the wet on wet method of painting watercolours would be the most suitable for painting water. But it is a haphazard method and the results can be unexpected. The surface of water might be better explained by carefully drawing and painting the objects in or around the area of water. The shape of pebbles and rocks above the surface can say a lot about the direction, depth and character of a stream or river.

Above: boats and their reflections in water are difficult to draw in a convincing way; their shapes present problems for many artists. It is often best to put aside preconceived ideas about specific shapes and to look at boats in abstract terms of form and colour. It's only after close and detailed observation that you begin to "see" the real appearance and structure of the boat you are drawing.

Low Tide, Southwold was painted by Charles Bartlett, whose motive for the watercolour was "The stillness and quality of light." The artist went on to say, "Compositionally, I decided to simplify the group of boats to focus the interest on one boat, also to have a larger, plain area of water to complement the complexity of the staging and mooring ropes. The colour is fairly subdued but is typical of East Anglian sea and landscape which has a quality of light which is peculiar to this part of the country." After making a pencil study of the scene and the reflections of the water, the artist finished the watercolour in the studio on 140lb Saunders NOT Cold Pressed watercolour paper. It measures 50 × 40cm (20 × 16in). The artist's sketches, notes and visual memory cultivated over many years of working along this stretch of coast, all contributed to making this a powerful and convincing watercolour.

FLOWERS

There are two basic approaches to painting flowers: the detailed, botanical style, and the more poetic approach which tries to capture the simple beauty of fresh flowers. Whether you paint a single flower, a bunch of wild flowers or a large flower arrangement, they make fascinating subject matter. It isn't necessary to have a large garden to paint flowers; visit a florist and purchase flowers to paint. But resist the temptation to buy flowers of every colour and shape and size — you need only a few to start.

Do not attempt at first to paint a "flower arrangement". Limit the amount of flowers, perhaps restricting yourself to a few of the same colour. Wild flowers, dried flowers and grasses look good in simple containers, such as a milk jug or, as in this still life (**right**) by the author, in a used French mustard pot. What remains of the red wax seal is a useful spot of bright colour in an otherwise quiet arrangement.

Left and above: Lucy Willis has painted these daffodils with a direct simple honesty, recapturing the original spontaneous delight that she found in the subject. The composition is helped by the two stabilizing shadows stretching across the table top.

Above, right and below: there is immense variety of colour and texture in Pamela Kay's paintings of flowers. Her pictures, as here, often include fruit, twigs and wild grasses, and are carefully set pieces. They have an honesty about them (although the arrangements can be large and complex), and a basic simplicity in the tradition of the great French still-life painter Chardin. The beauty and quality of the simplest basket, bowl or flower pot is painted with immense care.

If you want to paint a flower arrangement, gain confidence and experience by building up the painting flower by flower. Select a large, bright flower and draw and paint it a little off-centre. Now take a second flower, one that you feel would look good against the first; complete this one. Continue adding to your picture gradually, flower by flower, filling it in with small flowers and leaves, as the design evolves. In this way the picture is easy to handle. Because it develops slowly your painting is unlikely to go out of control but, as with other subjects, you must know when to stop.

LILY

Chris Jones

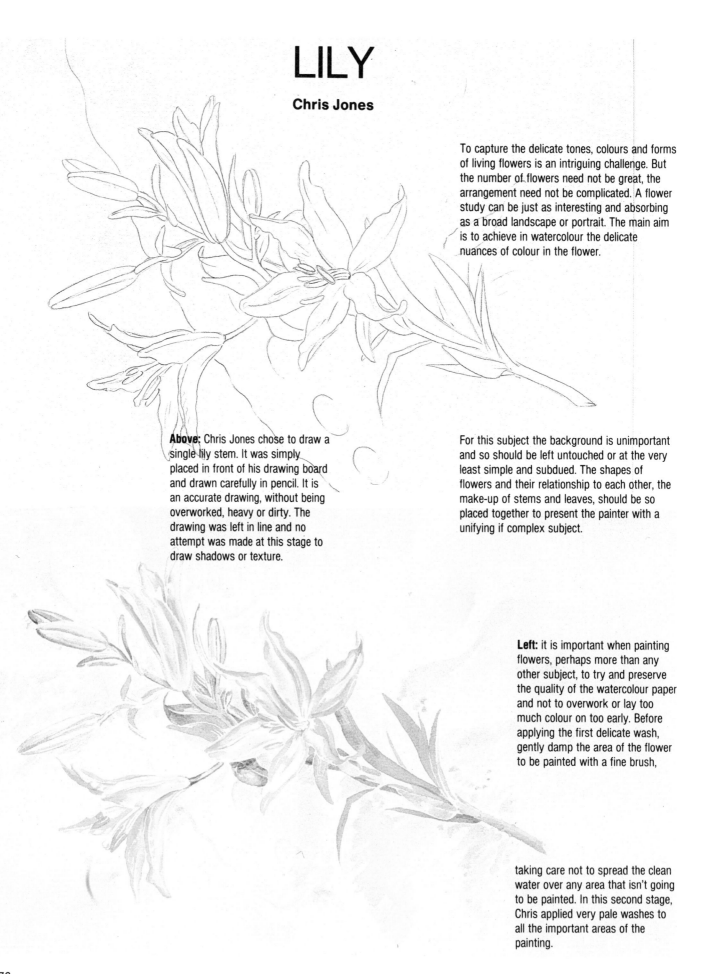

To capture the delicate tones, colours and forms of living flowers is an intriguing challenge. But the number of flowers need not be great, the arrangement need not be complicated. A flower study can be just as interesting and absorbing as a broad landscape or portrait. The main aim is to achieve in watercolour the delicate nuances of colour in the flower.

Above: Chris Jones chose to draw a single lily stem. It was simply placed in front of his drawing board and drawn carefully in pencil. It is an accurate drawing, without being overworked, heavy or dirty. The drawing was left in line and no attempt was made at this stage to draw shadows or texture.

For this subject the background is unimportant and so should be left untouched or at the very least simple and subdued. The shapes of flowers and their relationship to each other, the make-up of stems and leaves, should be so placed together to present the painter with a unifying if complex subject.

Left: it is important when painting flowers, perhaps more than any other subject, to try and preserve the quality of the watercolour paper and not to overwork or lay too much colour on too early. Before applying the first delicate wash, gently damp the area of the flower to be painted with a fine brush,

taking care not to spread the clean water over any area that isn't going to be painted. In this second stage, Chris applied very pale washes to all the important areas of the painting.

Right and below: the painting of the flowers was gradually built up from light to dark. Chris looked very carefully at the subject and gently applied slightly darker tones to the flowers while the first washes were still damp. Because these soft washes merged to form subtle, translucent effects, a hard-edged look was avoided. Second and third washes need to be absorbed without appearing thick and hard, and should dry without leaving a noticeable line. If the paint dries coarsely and unevenly, you can carefully dampen the area with clean fresh water and lift out some of the colour with a damp brush or cotton bud squeezed dry. You can do this only once or twice. After that, the area will become muddy and the surface of the paper will be destroyed. Any brush mark after that will look dark and be unmanageable. Your painting method needs to be logical in flower painting, and it should progress from the first simple pale areas of wash to as much delicate detail as possible, keeping the colour clean and positive all the time.

SPRING FLOWERS

Anne Maclaren

Anne Maclaren is constantly making notes, drawing, sketching and collecting ideas for her paintings. Windows are often incorporated into her paintings — they provide a useful framework in which she can work. Several vases were tried and rejected before the blue one was selected for this painting; and a number of roughs and sketches were done before the final arrangement was chosen. She always notes the direction of the light.

Right: first a careful pencil drawing was made on stretched watercolour paper. Both flowers and leaves were drawn very accurately. The location of the white flowers was important because here the white paper would remain unpainted and so the first drawing had to be accurate. An arrow, drawn in the top righthand corner indicates the direction of light.

Below left: a light wash of colour was placed on the background, and some of the green was allowed to bleed into the leaves. Then, blue was laid in on both the sky and the vase.

Below right: the background colour was softened with cotton buds while still wet. Pinks and purples were added to the flowers in light washes, keeping everything soft without too much finished detail. Care was taken all the time to prevent colour from covering the white flowers.

Above: the last stage is always difficult because it's a problem knowing when to stop but it is usually a mistake to even try to achieve photographic detail. The artist worked over the whole area of the painting, except for the white flowers, all the time keeping the colour very transparent and thin. The greatest depth of colour was applied to the vase, the focal point. When the artist decided to stop, she drew two coloured pencil lines around the painting which helped to complete and hold what is a soft, charming and subtle painting.

PAINTING PEOPLE

Painting people can mean not only painting a likeness but also taking into consideration people's surroundings and background and the circumstances in which you are painting them. Friends and members of your family make ideal models, as you know them well already. If you get to know your sitter, a more understanding portrait will follow. The watercolour should be not only a study of a human being but an individual impression of a character whose personality should become apparent in the painting.

The sitter's posture and clothes are an important factor in painting a portrait. They can say a lot about the character of the person you are trying to portray, and it may be that you will want to distort or give emphasis to them to portray certain characteristics. For example, a sitter might be a very colourful and extrovert person and this would be taken into consideration when adopting a style or approach to the subject. A quiet and introvert personality could equally be conveyed by painting in subdued and muted tones. As with most subjects, when you start to paint, look at your subject far more than you look at your unfinished painting.

Below left: Jacqueline Rizvi's portrait of a man reading is a portrait in an interior. As in many of her paintings, space and light are just as important as the subject.
Below: in this study of a very young baby, she has sketched a fleeting impression in light swift strokes of colour. A lengthy detailed painting would be not only impractical with such a subject but also unsuitable.

You will find that at one point, although the work seems far from finished, you have achieved a fleeting likeness; then a few brush strokes later it is lost. Knowing when to stop is difficult, but gradually you will learn to recognize the right moment.

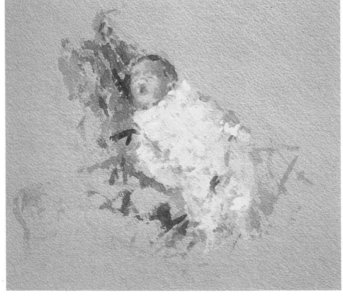

Left: ordinary, everyday domestic situations provide endless material for paintings that can be done quickly in the same place. The author painted his grandmother without her knowledge while she was engrossed in a book.

The portrait of his wife, however on the opposite page is more formally posed.

The painting by Jacqueline Rizvi of a figure by a window (**below**) is a remarkable composition — it breaks all the rules. The figure faces out of the picture, which doesn't normally help a composition, and the picture is divided into two equal parts, the figure and the view of the window. And yet it does succeed. The strength of the artist's vision ensures that the painting carries conviction.

Left: painting a self-portrait is always a useful exercise and it has the advantage of the model being free and always available. Arrange a mirror next to your working area so that you can watch yourself as you paint. Always try to be as honest as possible.

A CHILD IN DUNGAREES

Diana Johnson

Children are particularly difficult subjects to paint because they find it hard to stay in one place for any length of time, so it's necessary to paint and draw very quickly. It might be useful to paint them while they are occupied with a favourite toy or, better still, while they are asleep.

Here, the image was drawn freely, using a 2B pencil on a Bockingford watercolour pad. The drawing wasn't fixed because there may have been alterations later.

Diana Johnson usually works on themes that continue over a period of years. One such was a series of child portraits. She loves children and the way they dress, and follows their lives in her paintings. Having been drawn, photographed and documented, the children are now quite unselfconscious about sitting for their portraits.

The first colours were very pale. Diana Johnson uses watercolour blocks by Schmincke which are mixed on a china palette with purified water. She says, "in portraiture it's important that the colour is accurate." Great care was taken with the delicate skin tones.

Diana Johnson describes her working methods very simply: "Gradually the layers of colour go on, large brushes with small ones at the ready to fill in the tiny areas quickly; sometimes working on wet grounds, sometimes smudging with tissues, coming back with the pencil to discover a feature or to remind myself to colour in later or emphasize a form. I rub out most of the pencil as I go, but sometimes leave it in. As work dries I prop it up so that I can sit with a cup of tea and plan my next move."

She continues, "Knowing when a painting is finished is a difficult decision, mostly intuitive, sometimes logical. It becomes apparent because I am less and less willing to make more marks. Each area is completed to a required level in relation to the others of the composition. I think it over for a day or so. Some go straight to be framed, others into an old plan chest, and others into a folio to join the rest of the collection of drawings and paintings of children."

FIGURES FROM LIFE

Albany Wiseman

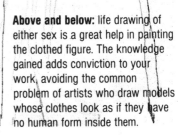

Anatomy

When painting the human figure, an understanding of the underlying structure is essential to give substance and authority to your work. Studying the human skeleton can help you not only to understand how the human figure works and is constructed but also to realize the proportions that make up the body. Familiarity with the main muscles, their functions and shapes, will add to your drawing and painting.

Above and below: life drawing of either sex is a great help in painting the clothed figure. The knowledge gained adds conviction to your work, avoiding the common problem of artists who draw models whose clothes look as if they have no human form inside them.

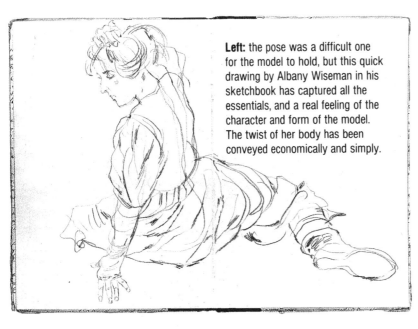

Left: the pose was a difficult one for the model to hold, but this quick drawing by Albany Wiseman in his sketchbook has captured all the essentials, and a real feeling of the character and form of the model. The twist of her body has been conveyed economically and simply.

Models

Local art clubs and classes are a good answer to the problem of recruiting a model because it is easier and cheaper to ask a model to pose for a group of artists. Models with plenty of character are often the most interesting to paint. People move, they breathe, sag and ache. It is this very fact that makes figure studies so fascinating.

Posing is boring and can be cold, so provide a comfortable environment, and ask the model to pose in a natural, simple way avoiding heroic, obscure, contrived and complex poses. Your model will need to rest and stretch at regular intervals, so mark the floor or chair indicating the exact position, with chalk.

Don't be afraid of readjusting and making alterations to your painting; redraw and repaint freely. In this way your work will improve. If you are self-satisfied and complacent your progress will be limited.

In the early stages of drawing a model, it can be helpful to reduce the image of the model to simple geometric shapes. This avoids overconcentration on detail which does nothing to explain the broader areas of the body. If time allows and the basics are right the details can then be added. Clothes have a character of their own which adds to the general impression of the character of the sitter.

PORTRAIT OF AN OLD LADY

Michael Whittlesea

When drawing and painting an elderly person, the comfort of the sitter is obviously important, and it was essential that this old lady was sitting comfortably and naturally. Time is also important: there is a limit to how long someone can sit reasonably still. So the decision was made to make the pose as simple as possible and to ensure that the sitter was warm and comfortable. Materials were laid out beforehand in order not to waste time.

Above: coloured masking liquid was painted over the area of the hair ensuring that, despite free handling of colour, the white of the hair would remain.

Using an HB pencil the main features and proportions were drawn in. Fixative wasn't used because this can affect a later application of watercolour.

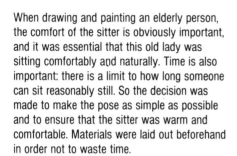

It's not easy to start on difficult areas such as the head and hands, so the dress was worked on instead, with a very diluted wash of manganese blue brushed over it (**above**). Thin washes of Payne's grey were applied to the jumper, cushion and background. It was now time to start the face and hands. A diluted wash of alizarin was brushed freely over this area. Yellow ochre was also added to parts of the background. The deep shadows on the face and hands were drawn in (**right**) with touches of manganese blue. Both ultramarine and Payne's grey were used to build up the tone behind the sitter's head and to help describe her weight and form. The masking liquid was then gently removed.

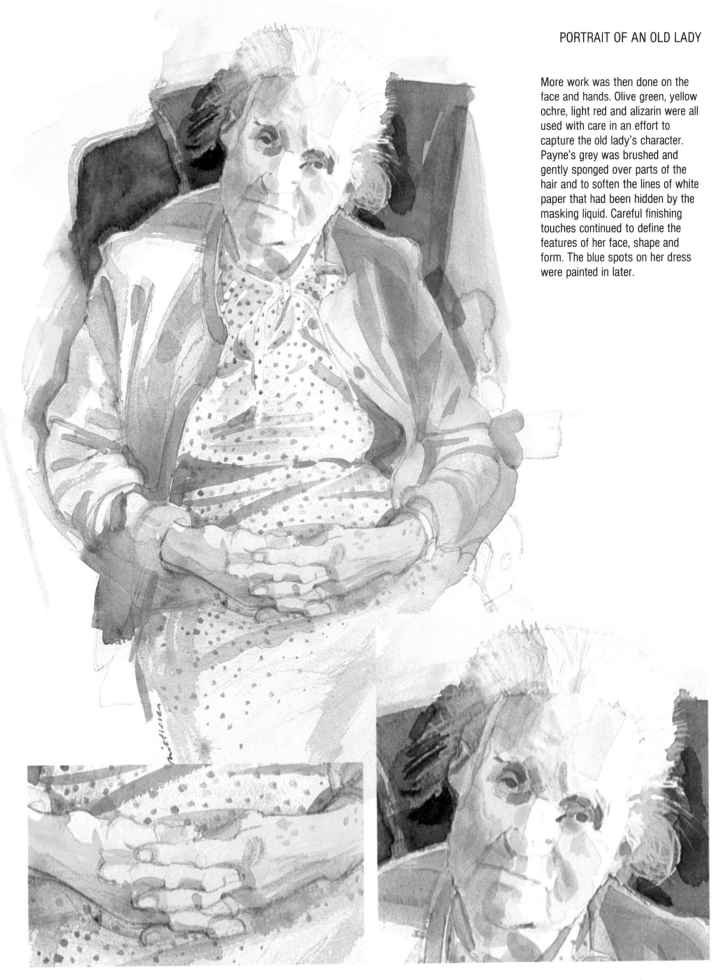

More work was then done on the face and hands. Olive green, yellow ochre, light red and alizarin were all used with care in an effort to capture the old lady's character. Payne's grey was brushed and gently sponged over parts of the hair and to soften the lines of white paper that had been hidden by the masking liquid. Careful finishing touches continued to define the features of her face, shape and form. The blue spots on her dress were painted in later.

STUDYING PEOPLE

Albany Wiseman

The Royal Regatta, held annually since 1923 at Henley-on-Thames, near London, is a good example of a colourful event which can provide good subject material for watercolour painting.

Painting groups of figures at what has been described as the biggest fancy dress party in the world, can produce a fascinating visual narrative of the event.

After making separate sketches and studies of an overall scene, it can be put together later in the studio where you can embark on a more finished, detailed work.

Above: these watercolour drawings were done by Albany Wiseman with great rapidity in a small sketch book. There wasn't time for laborious studies, and working in this way avoided drawing too much attention to himself. He identified the important facts and drew and painted them with energy and movement.

The charm and colour of this event and the atmosphere of an English summer, have been clearly expressed in the sketches.

It's difficult to draw exactly what one sees without resorting to preconceived ideas about the subject. The artist has looked hard at the shapes and movements of the figures.

Albany Wiseman put down his impressions with simple unfussy strokes. Time hasn't been wasted on too much detail but the figures have nonetheless been related to their setting.

Left and below: Albany Wiseman watched the boules players in France for a while before drawing these lively, simple, pencil sketches. There is a feeling of movement in these images as well as of the individual characters of the players.

The pencil drawings (**above**) were later translated into these watercolours (**below**). The best and most expressive drawings were selected, and then arranged and redrawn in watercolour, in an economical style.

BUILDINGS

Simple perspective is needed for most paintings of buildings or townscapes, as is the ability to draw. This is more essential for buildings than for many other subjects; no amount of tricks or techniques will help if the drawing and proportions are incorrect. Architectural subjects need patience and careful preliminary drawings. Despite these drawbacks, the shapes, patterns and textures of buildings and their relationship to their surroundings provide good material for watercolours.

Buildings are usually covered in detail — it's one of the things that makes them so interesting. But in the early stages of painting it is a good idea to avoid elaboration. Aim rather at giving the feeling of a solid simple structure. Details and decoration can be added easily at a later stage. Begin by making a simple drawing, using line to draw the main angles. The shapes and proportions need to be carefully considered and drawn. When the perspective and proportions are mostly correct, the main shadows should be indicated. Try to avoid drawing in the shadows with heavy pencil, just indicate their perimeters; watercolour on pencil can become dirty and grey.

Below: in towns and cities, large buildings block out sunlight, whole areas are left in shadow, and narrow winding streets, passageways and doorways not only provide contrasts in scale but provide dramatic compositions of light and dark.

Left: rather than attempt to draw the whole of a building it may be more rewarding to take a detail, such as a doorway or window, and explore all its possibilities. The window with the single pot of flowers was worth drawing, and it had an additional area of interest in the extraordinary shadow cast by the torn blind. This idea was noted and sketched and later drawn up and painted in the studio.

Left: it's often impractical to set up an easel in strong sunlight or in a crowded street. This is where a sketchbook really comes into its own. It's possible to wedge yourself into a shady corner or sit at a café table and draw undisturbed. These drawings and notes can later be translated into larger paintings.

Above left: the texture of the stonework of the church and the wall, and the prickly needle-like leaves of the gorse and evergreens, have been superbly caught in this quick drawing and will serve as an excellent record of the scene when the artist comes to paint it.

Above: this watercolour of buildings near the Piazza San Marco in Venice was painted not because they are a famous landmark but more because of the dramatic light which appeared to fall on only a small proportion of the view. More than fifty per cent of the building is completely in shadow; the colours of the buildings in the sunlight are soft and subtle.

Left: another view of Venice, with the Rialto Bridge in the background, also contrasts buildings as well as water flooded with sunlight with other areas in shadow. But the muted greys, siennas and yellows make the contrast a subtle one.

ST MARTIAL IN SUMMER

Juliette Palmer

The subject matter of many of Juliette Palmer's watercolours is the picturesque. She takes great pleasure in finding new places to paint and draw, and chooses ever more complicated views. "I stalk about, climb high or crouch low to obtain the most exciting composition and to cause plants, rocks or roots to loom large, cut across and break up the picture space", she says. Juliette feels that by transferring her vision of sunlit landscapes, villages or gardens into paintings, the pleasure of the original scene is prolonged, and she wants to pass on that exhilaration to others.

After transferring the drawing onto watercolour paper, colour was applied slowly and carefully. Juliette Palmer cannot resist putting detail in every part of the picture. However, the vital structure of the composition, its overall lights, shades and contrast, its unity, all have to be retained in her mind.

The artist makes a careful drawing with colour notes written in. Drawings and notes made in summer are used by the artist when she works in her studio in winter.

Although the artist enjoys calm simplicity in other artists' work, she doesn't allow it in her own.

She painted various parts of the picture as the fancy took her, covering the picture in colour gradually and in a random fashion.

In some areas colour washes are laid on quite roughly because they would be changed later. These washes "knock back" the starkness of the white paper where it was definitely not wanted.

Juliette Palmer

In the completing stages, in order to avoid the mistake of running colour over a precious bright or pale area, the artist worked carefully bit by bit. She applied pale washes first and gradually built up darker areas. Only very occasionally does she resort to adding process white or wetting and lifting the colour off by blotting. Throughout the work the paint was never allowed to become muddy or obscure the translucence of the white paper shining through the watercolour.

HOUSE ON THE HILL

Michael Whittlesea

A painting of a building or the urban landscape needs believable, solid drawing. Everything needs to be considered and placed; the building should look as if it has solid foundations. This subject needs time and perseverance, so try to find a secluded viewpoint where it is possible to settle down, draw and observe it. Architectural details are interesting, but the priority should be a convincing basic structure. The details can be indicated later, simply and without elaboration.

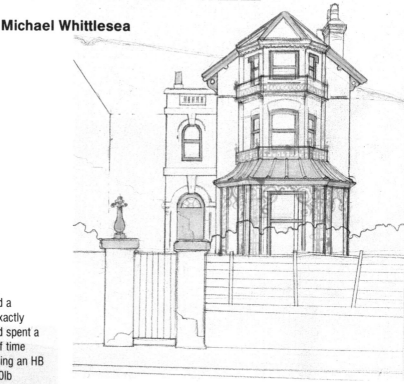

Right: the author found a comfortable position exactly opposite the house and spent a considerable amount of time drawing the subject using an HB pencil on stretched 140lb watercolour paper.

Above: when the drawing seemed to be reasonably satisfactory, coloured masking fluid was painted on the windows, roof, decorative ironwork, the door and chimney. Then, as soon as the marking fluid had dried, a generous mixture of diluted Naples yellow and manganese blue was washed over the area of the sky.

Above: next, a thin mixture of Naples yellow and Payne's grey was washed over the rest of the painting. When both of these washes had dried a mix of ultramarine, viridian and alizarin was painted onto the windows and roof.

Above: the whole painting was allowed to dry before a dark mixture of ultramarine, alizarin and Naples yellow was brushed freely onto the background areas. Again, when this wash had dried, yellow ochre was applied to the façade of the house, and allowed to sink into parts of the background colour. While the background was still wet ultramarine and raw sienna were also painted on it, in washes. At this stage the masking fluid was rubbed off so that the final detail and colour could be added.

MECHANICAL OBJECTS

Dennis Roxby Bott

We are surrounded by mechanical objects, and use them every day, but it's not often that they are used by artists as subjects for watercolour painting. Mechanical objects are probably better to draw and paint when they have been well used, and when rust and decay have set in — it softens the look of machinery. Old cars seem more interesting than new ones and a rotting wooden boat is more appealing to draw than a perfectly new, glass fibre one. The setting and surroundings can also help to produce an interesting painting rather than a mechanical drawing. Good drawing is important for this subject and the object should look as if it could, or did work. One of the great advantages is that old mechanical objects do not move unexpectedly. You can return to the theme and draw and paint for long periods of time.

Left and below: Dennis Roxby Bott likes to discover and paint unusual sights such as this Rolls Royce car in a crumbling barn. The artist had used the patchwork quality of the old barn to split the painting into sections. There is a convincing feeling of recession, and the composition leads the eye directly to the main centre of interest, focusing attention on the Rolls Royce. Even so, relating the subject to its setting is an important factor in the painting's success. The artist used a fairly hard pencil to map very carefully and precisely the details of the car. When the drawing was complete a very delicate palette was used to convey the soft light that fell on the Rolls Royce through the openings in the barn.

Left: the old barn and wooden farm wagon is a very linear subject. Dennis used a very delicate pencil drawing to which a strong design of horizontals and verticals was added; it was painted in delicately at an early stage.

Below: applying the colour was a time-consuming process because precise tones were required, and each wash had to dry before the next one was laid next to it. The process may have been slow, but the subject wasn't going to move, and this allowed the artist to spend as much time as necessary on it.

ANIMALS

Animals and birds are excellent subjects for watercolours; feathers, scales and fur provide colour, pattern and textural variations. An understanding of animals will help you to paint them convincingly. Drawing them constantly in their own surroundings and studying their behaviour will add realism to your work. Watercolours are very suitable for this purpose because they are easily portable so that you can position yourself near to the animal. Like most children they will not stay still for very long so work quickly and directly.

A good way to start drawing and painting animals is to draw your own pets. They are used to you and there will be times when they are around the house or garden sitting or sleeping. Explore various working methods to convey their character, texture and movements. If you are drawing animals elsewhere, working in a small sketch book might provoke less curiosity than a large drawing board will. It might seem easier to draw stuffed animals, but although this can be helpful, drawings and paintings of stuffed animals tend to look over-finished and artificial. If you use photographs for reference you must try to understand the underlying structure of the animals and draw it. Otherwise the result will be unconvincing.

Left and below: Charlotte Halliday loves cats, and these delightful studies drawn in a small sketch book convey that love and affection. She has varied her methods from fine pencil to watercolour; some are detailed, others simply drawn in with a brush. The result is a very observant and knowledgeable portrait of a cat.

Below left: this small watercolour by the author demonstrates that it isn't necessary to draw every hair and whisker to suggest the form of a cat.

Quick pencil sketches are an excellent way to explore and study the shape, characteristics and behaviour of animals. Draw animals in as many different positions as you can. Eating, sleeping and sitting animals will provide material for a number of small studies. When the animal moves, start another drawing.

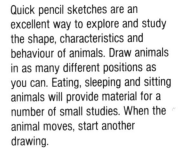

Most animals, especially cows and sheep, will be inquisitive of your presence at first, but if you stay still and quiet they will become used to you and eventually will ignore you.

As with figures, the structures and shapes of animals can be reduced to various geometrical forms — cubes, spheres, cylinders and cones — and specific proportions. At first, ignore the complicated details and concentrate on the main shapes. The resulting drawing won't have photographic detail, but it will enable you to draw convincingly the likeness and character of a particular animal.

Projecting bones are important points of reference and should be noted and understood. Also, some domestic animals are sturdy and heavily built, and can be drawn to contrast with those which have to move quickly and whose legs are designed for flexibility and speed.

Try working on several sketches at once. Animals tend to return to the same position to eat or when cleaning themselves and even if a drawing is incomplete when the animal moves, the chances are that it will come back to a similar position and you can then continue with that drawing.

GALLOPING RACEHORSES

Diana Johnson

It is very satisfying to make a successful painting of the human figure, but to add to it movement and a subject such as galloping horses is an even greater achievement. This combination can only be successfully achieved with an intimate knowledge and love of horses and many hours of observation and drawing. Using a mixture of references is the best approach. On-the-spot drawings and good photographs can be used, but too much reliance on photographs can result in a frozen, stiff image; not the feeling you want to impart when you are painting a subject with so much movement and colour. So, identify the main shapes and use a free, experimental style, with quick brush strokes. This will be more effective than a highly detailed painting, however accomplished it is. The end result should be fresh and vigorous.

Diana Johnson sits in her kitchen during the winter, working on paintings and using drawings and photographs taken during the summer months. Some of the studies and reference she uses go back many years. She has an intimate knowledge of horses because she has been closely associated with them for most of her life — their training, hunting, racing, exercising and shoeing, and in recent years, even stunt work.

First, she draws up the idea freely in pencil (**above**). Surrounded by reference and photographs, she works on five or six paintings at once. This allows her time to think between stages and while waiting for washes to dry.

Left: the first areas of colour are pale and set the mood for the rest of the painting.

Right: gradually the layers of colour go on, applied with large brushes but with small ones at the ready to fill in the tiny areas quickly. Sometimes Diana works on wet grounds, sometimes smudging the colour with tissues, or coming back with the pencil to point up a feature or to remind herself to colour a bit in later or to emphasize a form. She rubs out most of the pencil as she goes, but sometimes leaves it in for added effect.

Below: although she is unable to anticipate the exact end result, her instinct makes her less and less willing to make any more marks. She then thinks it over for a day or two, before putting it in the folio or sending it to the framers.

PHEASANT

Chris Jones

Birds are an absorbing subject, but drawing and painting them in their natural environment is obviously difficult and although visual notes of observations are possible, detailed studies can be done only with dead or caged birds. The pattern and arrangement of feathers is complex and needs to be drawn with care and a certain amount of knowledge of the underlying structure of the bird; for example, where the wing joins the shoulder. The markings on the feathers have a characteristic rhythm, and it is useful to count the number of feathers on a wing. At first, the feathers might seem too numerous to evaluate, but if you take a little time to analyse the bird in this way, it will enable you to draw and paint it with conviction.

Left: Chris Jones has carefully drawn the bird with a minimum of background. The shape and markings on the pheasant are so exciting that a fussy background would only detract. A straightforward simple view of the bird was chosen, and drawn with a reasonably hard pencil in great detail. The groupings of the feathers needed to be clearly defined at the start. If this had not been done, trying to sort out the groups of feathers later in paint would have been not only a confusing but also a hopeless task.

Below left: the first neutral washes were laid on the background and allowed to dry before the pattern of all the markings was carefully painted in.

Left: a little more definition was added to the background. The cool blues used in the background washes have helped to make this area recede and the warmer colours used on the bird have emphasized its solid form, pulling it forward in space.

Above: careful analysis of the pheasant continued as the shadows and each feather and its colour changes were considered and painted. The shadow under the bird was strengthened to finish the painting.

Top right: the blue string was introduced to provide a sharp clear note of bright blue. Although the picture is highly detailed and worked, much of the lighter markings are left untouched with the watercolour paper showing through.

CAT ON A SOFA

Anne Maclaren

Watercolour is a particularly good medium for drawing and painting animals, and domestic animals make very good models. Cats, for example, sleep a great deal. Their markings make wonderful patterns which can echo the colours and shapes found in carpets and cushions. Watercolour is ideal for conveying the appearance of fur. Sketchbooks are convenient for drawing domestic animals in relation to their surroundings and will provide ideas and material for future paintings.

After making many preliminary sketches to determine the composition, the artist decided to make a very accurate drawing showing exactly where the white areas were, so that they could be preserved during the progressive stages of painting. The direction of the light was also noted.

Light washes of colour were applied, kept loose with plenty of water. The whole picture was considered, and each area related in colour and pattern to the next. Nothing was overworked or finished.

The detail was gradually built up, concentrating on the focal point — the cat. It's important to remember that you can create depth of colour by laying many washes always working from light to dark.

The problem at this stage was to avoid overworking the painting, as the freshness in watercolours is lost easily. You have to gradually build up the colour without it becoming muddy. When the decision was made to stop, the whiskers were drawn in with white gouache.

MOUNTING AND FRAMING

Spend some time thinking about how you are going to mount/mat and frame your watercolour because paintings take on a very different look when they are mounted/matted and framed. When choosing a frame make sure that the colour and style of the frame reflect the character, style and colours of the painting. I prefer to spend my time painting and leave framing to an expert, but many artists prefer to cut their own mounts/mats and frame their own paintings.

Before you cut a watercolour off the drawing board make sure that it is thoroughly dry. Cut the opposite edges of the paper, rather than working around it in a clockwise or anticlockwise fashion, then trim the edges so that they are square.

Sheets of mounting board/mat of varying thickness are available in a variety of colours. Light or neutral colours are generally more suitable for the subtlety of watercolours, whereas darker shades tend to overpower them, unless of course, the colours in your painting are particularly strong. So, put different coloured sheets behind your painting to see what effect they have, before making a final decision.

You could also decorate a plain mount/mat with lines or stripes of watercolour or coloured ink to complement the colours in the painting; this is done with a ruling pen.

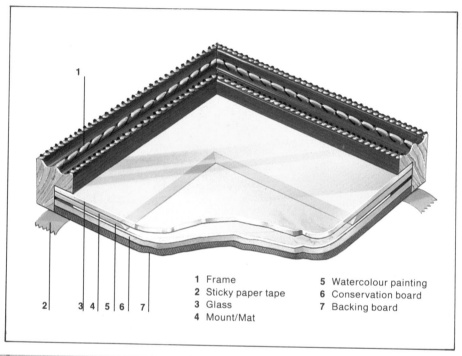

1 Frame
2 Sticky paper tape
3 Glass
4 Mount/Mat
5 Watercolour painting
6 Conservation board
7 Backing board

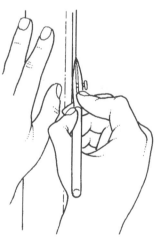

A plain mount/mat can be decorated with fine lines of watercolour or ink. Fill one third of a ruling pen with the colour, and adjust the pen to the required line width. Draw the line against a steel rule with a bevelled edge.

Right: a single mount/mat in a neutral colour often suits a painting in which the colours are soft and muted. The edges of the mount/mat define the shape of the painting and help to contain the diffused colours.

Once you have selected the mount/mat, consider the size and content of your painting. A small image, or a painting with a dramatic perspective, are often offset well by a large mount/mat, and may look more interesting if they are placed off-centre. Larger paintings, or those with a close-up viewpoint, often look good with a narrow margin to frame them. If you want to centre your painting, remember to leave a wider margin of mount/mat at the bottom than at the top, otherwise it will look as if it is sinking into the frame.

Mounting/matting and framing can be carried out with very straightforward and inexpensive equipment, and not too much skill is needed. Where you will need some practice, however, is in mitring the corners of the frame so that they fit together exactly. If you are anxious about mitring frames yourself, the shop you bought them from will usually do this for you. There are also some very good do-it-yourself framing kits available with ready-mitred corners.

Right: in this case the added "weight" of a double mount/mat of the same colour balances the painting which itself is heavier in colour and content. The shadows of the edges of the two mounts/mats create a sort of double frame around the painting which does not detract from the painting in any way.

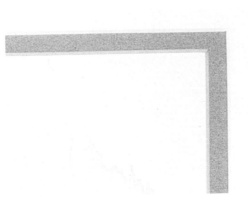

Right: the decorative finish created by a double mount/mat of contrasting colours can often complement a simple painting.

Paintings do not necessarily have to be framed singly. Often, if they have a similar theme, as these seascapes do, they can enhance each other's qualities and reinforce the theme by being framed as a single unit.

GLOSSARY

Airbrush
A tool which is filled with liquid watercolour or ink, and, when connected to an air compressor, releases a fine spray which is good for creating graduated tones of colour. With the help of stencils and paper cut out masks, a high degree of finish and detail can be obtained. These qualities make the airbrush a very suitable technique for commercial illustration.

Aquarelle
A work of art painted in watercolour or a drawing tinted with washes of a waterbased pigment.

Atmosphere
In painting, "atmosphere" relates to the feeling of space and distance between the foreground and the background.

Botanical painting
The study, drawing and painting of trees and plants.

Brushes
The best watercolour brushes are made from sable. Synthetic brushes are a poor substitute.

Complementary colours
Any colour is complementary to the colour with which it contrasts most strongly, as red with green, yellow with violet, blue with orange. Complementary colours occur opposite each other on the conventional colour wheel.

Composition
The satisfactory placing and arrangement of the various shapes and colours in a painting or drawing.

Cool colours
The quality and "temperature" of a colour. Blue for example is a very cool colour. As a general rule cool colours recede.

Dry brush technique
A technique using a virtually dry brush, the water having been squeezed out. The pigment is brushed or even rubbed over a textured surface leaving a granulated effect.

Earth colours
Pigments obtained from minerals and clay such as ochre, umber and sienna. The colours produced are less intense than synthetic colours.

Ferrule
The metal part of a paint brush which holds the hairs in place.

Figurative
A painting which contains figures. This term is sometimes used to describe any non-abstract painting.

Fixative
A thin varnish which can be sprayed onto pencil drawings which prevents fading or accidental rubbing off.

Fugitive
Colours which fade due to defects or when exposed to strong sunlight.

Gouache
Known as "body colour" or "designers' colour". Basically a watercolour made opaque. It dries with a matt, dry, surface.

Ground
Any surface on which a painting is to be painted.

Gum strip
Brown paper adhesive tape used to attach watercolour paper to a drawing board.

Half tones
The colours or tones between the extremes of very light or very dark.

Hatching and Crosshatching
A technique where parallel lines are drawn to create an effect of density. Lines drawn in the opposite direction, covering the original lines produce the effect known as "crosshatching"

Highlight
An important point in a painting produced by the white paper being left blank, or when white is added over a darker colour.

Impasto
Paint built up to produce a heavy texture. Pure watercolour is unsuitable for this technique, but Gouache can be used to produce this effect.

Life drawing
Drawing from the nude model.
"Working from life" can be a general
term for drawing and painting
anything directly observed.

Line drawing
A drawing made up of fine or thick
lines. Shadows or half tones are
not used.

Liquid watercolours
Pigments supplied in bottles. Even
when diluted, liquid watercolours
can be very intense and sometimes
even luminous.

Masking and masking fluid
This technique is used to protect
an existing colour or an area of
white paper when subsequent colours
are laid over them. The mask or the
masking liquid is peeled or rubbed
away when the overpainting is dry.

Medium
This term can refer to a particular
painting process, for example
watercolour is a painting medium.
It is also used as a term for
additives such as oil, wax or
varnish.

Modelling
Painting and drawing to give the
impression of solidity and to
express areas of light and shade.

Monochrome
A work of art painted in only one
colour. This is usually black or
brown mixed with white or used in
a diluted form.

NOT
A type of watercolour paper that
falls between the smooth surfaced
papers and the heavily textured
rough papers.

Opaque
Pigment which can obscure the
colour or surface of the paper
on which it is applied.

Palette
A term which not only refers to
the surface on which an artist
mixes his colours but can also
mean the range and choice of colours
for the artist.

Perspective
Methods of representing the
impression of depth and recession
on a flat surface. Linear
perspective makes use of parallel
lines and a vanishing point to
which the lines converge. Aerial
perspective suggests distance by
use of tones.

Pigment
Pigments are made from natural or
synthetic substances and can when
mixed with water and a binder
provide colour for painting.

Sepia
A cool brown ink or watercolour
often used for sketches and studies.

Spattering
Applying paint by flicking pigment
from the bristles of a stiff brush.
This is commonly done by running a
finger across the bristles.

Still Life
Painting a group of objects which
does not include figures.

Stippling
Dotting with the point of a brush.
"Stipple" has a similar effect.

Texture
The tactile appearance and feel of
a painted surface.

Tone
The degrees of light to dark are
measured on a scale of gradation
from black to white and referred to
as dark, light, mid to half tones.
Colours can be dark or light in
tone and so have a tonal value.

Underpainting
The basic elements of the painting
are sketched in. These early marks
are often covered up by later
applications of paint.

Wash
Diluted watercolour which can be
applied with either a large brush
or a sponge.

Watermark
The papermaker's name is often
incorporated in sheets of high
quality watercolour paper and can
be seen as a watermark when the
paper is held up to the light.

Wet in wet
Any watercolour technique which
involves the artist adding paint
to an already wet surface.

INDEX

PICTURE CREDITS